MW01050757

Creative Ropecraft

A brandy bottle covered in 4.5mm dia. three-strand hemp line.

A needlehitched flask in light blue and black three-strand twine. The cap is covered with a Turk's Head in 4.5mm dia. braided nylon and the neck carries a Turk's Head in nylon twine.

Three table lamps, wooden bases covered in *(left)* 4.5mm dia. braided nylon; *(centre)* 6.0mm dia. three-strand sisal; *(right)* 4.5mm dia. three-strand hemp. The method of base construction and working is described in detail for the design of the left-hand lamp shown here.

Creative Ropecraft

STUART E. GRAINGER

W · W · NORTON & COMPANY · INC ·

New York

Acknowledgment

I must express my appreciation of the help and advice so kindly
provided by my friend Clifford Ramsden in preparing the
photographs for this book.

Copyright © 1975 by G. Bell & Sons Ltd.
All Rights Reserved
First Edition

Library of Congress Cataloging in Publication Data

Grainger, Stuart E
   Creative ropecraft.

   Bibliography: p.
   Includes index.
   1. Fancy work. 2. Rope. 3. Knots and splices.
I. Title.
TT840.G63   1977   746'.04'71   76-49142
ISBN 0-393-08746-8
Printed in the United States of America.

1 2 3 4 5 6 7 8 9 0

Contents

A coffee jar, covered in three-strand 2.7mm dia. flax line with, from the top, a Crowned Star, Turk's Head, three grommets and a horizontal and vertical Turk's Head around the cap; a Star Knot, Crown Sennit background and two Wall and Crown knots, one in a vertical plane and the other horizontal.

(extreme left, below) The author's knife, covered in various flax lines with Crown Sennit and Needlehitched background, Turk's Head, Star Knot and Wall and Crown Knot.

(centre and right, below) Typical Bell Lanyards with Crown Sennit background. The knot combinations are detailed in the text and include Diamond, Star, Matthew Walker, Wall and Crown, Rose and Hangman's knots.

Introduction

During the Napoleonic wars British ships sailed to and fro for months on end, patrolling the same stretch of water on blockade duty, yet the hundreds of men on board had no television, no radio, no records and no magazines. There would have been a few simple musical instruments, but, for the vast majority, the only materials available to occupy their hands and minds in recreation were the discarded cordage and canvas from the ship's rigging and sails. This book is an introduction to the practical folk art which developed at sea in sailing ships, among the simplest and poorest of men, whose only skill, apart from that of personal survival, lay in their hands and the use of shipboard materials. Few of these men could write or read, yet they often spent years in cramped quarters aboard the same ship and, although frequently overworked, they also had to pass long periods of enforced inactivity, becalmed or at anchor, awaiting a berth or a favourable wind. The severely practical techniques employed in working and maintaining the ship's gear were used, modified and adapted in countless variations for making and, above all, for decorating small personal items such as knives, telescopes, needle cases, work baskets, sea chests and the like.

As sail gave way to steam, the way of life aboard ship changed: seamen were better educated, and more sophisticated pastimes became available, the practice of ropecraft for its own sake declined, and many of the practical knots, upon which men's lives once depended, were no longer needed. For more than half a century now sailing ships have been the exception rather than the rule in almost every trade, and there is a real danger of many of the old knots and techniques with cordage being forgotten and lost. Ship's officers wrote manuals of seamanship and ship handling, some of which contained details of the more important practical knots, but the really expert practitioners of the art, the able seamen and petty officers, were almost invariably illiterate, and certainly did not write books; the result is a general lack of literature on the subject.

Many basic practical knots are still in use, of course, and are too important to be allowed to disappear so long as there are fishermen and yachtsmen, who are among the very few continuing users of ordinary rope on a large scale. The difficulty about preserving the more specialized and ancient knots is that they no longer have a commercial value in the trade which developed them. It is not enough to illustrate and record them in print, nor to preserve a few handsome museum specimens, because this will not enable them to live any more than an Egyptian mummy lives. Most of the very old knots no longer used have a clear beauty, which is often found in utilitarian objects whose shape has been refined by evolution to produce the best results from the simplest form. These beautiful ancient knots, together with the purely or primarily decorative use of cordage, are the most likely to disappear, yet they provide a fascinating, useful and inexpensive hobby, deserving wider attention, but virtually unknown to many experts and teachers of other closely allied handicrafts, such as basketwork, weaving, crochet and macramé.

The aim of this book is to stimulate interest in the subject, outside as well as within the seafaring fraternity, and to provide a source of technical information sufficiently wide to feed the imagination of those whose interest is aroused, yet not so deep as to mystify or confuse. The drawings, all of which have been made from actual samples, are intended to convey the techniques, as far as possible without additional written instruction and, particularly in the early stages, great care has been taken to illustrate clearly each successive step in the tying of a knot. The text consists mainly of notes upon the use of the illustrated knots and techniques, rather than upon the process of tying them.

The reader is urged to understand and remember that this book only attempts to introduce the subject, which has many fascinating specialized branches worthy of further research. This is certainly not a comprehensive study in depth, although a few of the knots and techniques described are believed to be hitherto unpublished. Sennits have been dealt with only superficially and the same may be said of Turk's Heads, but two separate books could be written on these subjects alone.

Square Knotting, otherwise known as Macramé, is not mentioned, let alone discussed, because it has become a separate entity, an art in its own right, with a full and adequate literature to describe it, as a few minutes in any public library will prove.

Some basic information about modern cordage is provided here, and there is one chapter devoted to a selection of simple but important practical knots, most of which every Boy Scout is supposed to know, but these are in the nature of tools, for use with the more sophisticated and perhaps more interesting techniques discussed later.

The sailors of the past did not have the use of modern brightly coloured plastic cordage, which adds greatly to the scope of this subject as a hobby. We also have the modern benefit of self-adhesive tapes and handy, quick-drying, transparent glue in tubes, the use of which removes much of the time-consuming routine involved in seizing strands together and whipping the ends to prevent fraying, all of which had to be done with twine in the days of sailing ships.

The designs and methods of making specific articles, described towards the end of this book, have been developed as projects which, for the most part, can be taken up and put down as convenience and inclination dictate. Most of them can be completed in the space of an hour or two and they can be varied, doubtless also improved upon, according to the taste, skill and imagination of the individual and the variety of his or her materials.

1 *Cordage characteristics — standard knots*

Knots can be tied in a great many materials, such as leather, straw, cane and ribbon, but the material which is probably best for the purpose is that which has been evolved through centuries for holding things together—rope and twine.

Twine developed first, partly because things usually start small, but also because there are so many uses for twine, or string, as it is often called. Rope is really only twine made much bigger, but to make it so requires more strength and skill, and ingenious machines do most of the work these days.

Twine, in its simplest form, is just fibres of a suitable material, such as dried grass, animal hairs or wool, twisted together, so as to make a continuous length. The longer the fibres are, the better they hold together, and the better and stronger the twine is. The thinner and more flexible the fibres are, the easier the twine is to work with.

Rope has to be rather more complicated, but the most common kind is made also by twisting fibres together, quite loosely at first, into ropeyarns. The ropeyarns are then twisted together into strands, which are then twisted, or to use the correct term, 'laid', together in the opposite direction. In most rope, the yarns in the strands are twisted anti-clockwise, or left-handed, and the strands, usually three of them, are laid together clockwise, or right-handed and the two different directions of twist interact to keep the yarns firmly in place and give the rope a certain amount of elasticity.

Some ropes and twines are made by plaiting strands together, which makes

10

them flexible and easy to use, particularly for decorative knots, but they are rather more expensive, because they are more difficult to make, and they are much more difficult to join by splicing than are ordinary ropes.

It is always worth considering carefully what kind of line to choose for a particular purpose, and these days there are many types to choose from. First of all, the line must be strong enough. If you want it to be very strong, a man-made fibre, like nylon or Terylene, would probably be a good choice, but bear in mind that these materials are very springy and will stretch a long way before breaking. Some man-made fibres, particularly polypropylene, deterio- rate very quickly in sunlight, so should not be used for work intended to remain permanently in the open air. Some artificial fibres such as polyethylene are used to make very light-weight rope, which will float, but these are usually less strong than other materials.

For purely decorative ropework, flexibility, texture and colour are more important than strength. Plaited line is usually easy to work with, if you can afford it. Cotton is soft and can be dyed to produce almost any colour you like, but it does get dirty rather quickly. Polyethylene and polypropylene lines have been cheap for some years, although whether they will remain so must be problematical; these materials are easily washed and are available in a wide range of bright colours, but they can be rather difficult to work with, although this varies a great deal from one type to another.

Sources of supply for these ropes and twines vary almost as widely as the materials themselves. Heavier types of rope are not generally available on the retail market, except in yacht chandlers, which normally stock many different kinds of ropes and twine, but because they are expected to be strong and to withstand outdoor use in difficult conditions, most of the lines sold by yacht chandlers are quite expensive. For purely decorative ropework it is worth investigating many possible sources of material. Hardware stores often stock a number of inexpensive lines for clothes lines, gardening shops offer a variety of twines, Do-it-yourself shops, craft and needlework shops, Woolworths, haberdashers and, by no means least, local market stalls all offer rich potential. Finally, do not be put off by materials which do not appear attractive in the shop. Consider them carefully for texture, even if the colour is uninteresting. Remember how attractive those green glass fishing floats look when covered in tarry twine netting, yet a roll of the twine by itself appears most uninviting.

Just as there are different kinds of line for every purpose, so there are many different knots for use in various situations, indeed there are many thousands of knots and each profession that uses rope or twine has a few of its own. The sailor has probably produced more special knots than any other calling, but

ROPE

right hand lay

three strands

ropeyarns.

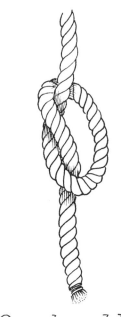

Overhand Knot.

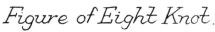

Figure of Eight Knot.

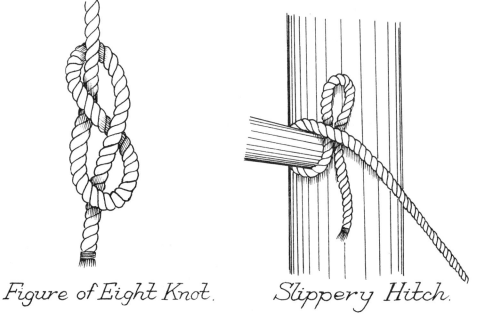

Slippery Hitch.

farmers, steeplejacks, circus hands and weavers, among many others, have all contributed their share to the general store of available knots. Only a strictly limited number of the most useful and best known knots are described here.

Knots are conveniently separated into three groups by their normal use and only one of these groups is properly called Knots; the other two are Bends and Hitches. Bends are used to tie the end of one rope to that of another, often of a different size and material. Hitches are used for tying a rope to something quite different, such as a tree, a rail, a ring, or to the bight (that is a loop somewhere along the length) of another rope. Knots are really only tied in the length of the rope itself, without direct application to anything else. The correct name of a knot will often tell you exactly what it was originally for, but that does not mean there is only one use for it. A good example is the Cow Hitch, which was and still is used by farmers to tie a cow or any other animal to a post, but the same Hitch has many other uses and sailors often use it in the form of a Bale Hitch or Sling Hitch, because they use it for slinging bales of cargo.

The Overhand Knot
The simplest knot of all, called the Overhand Knot, probably evolved hundreds of thousands of years ago and may well have been used to string beads, perhaps pretty shells, coloured stones or seeds on a string of hair. The only real use of the Overhand Knot is as a stopper knot, that is to stop the line pulling through a hole in something.

The Figure of Eight Knot
This is a much better stopper knot than the Overhand Knot, because, being bigger, it does the job better; also it is much easier to untie when pulled tight.

Round Turn and Two Half Hitches
A really good Hitch, but it must be made properly. Sometimes the full round turn is omitted and just two half hitches made, but this is not as good because the half hitches can be jammed against the post or bollard if the rope is pulled hard. It is also important that the half hitches are made in the same way, that is with the rope moving in the same direction around itself. Use this Hitch if in doubt about using any other, particularly when the direction of pull is likely to change, as when mooring a boat or tethering an animal.

Grocer's Hitch
This is a slip-knot, one that will slip along the twine, allowing adjustment around a parcel. The Grocer's Hitch is really a sliding Figure of Eight Knot. It

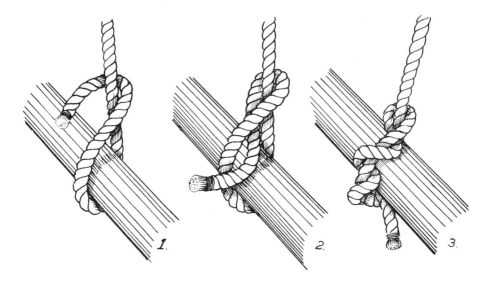

Timber Hitch.

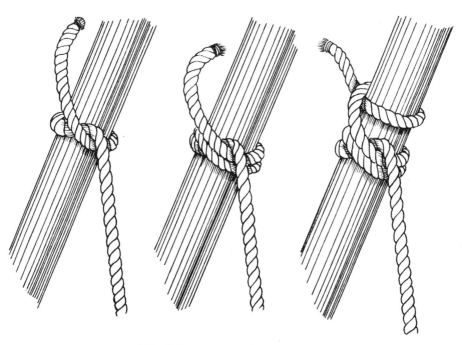

Rolling Hitch.

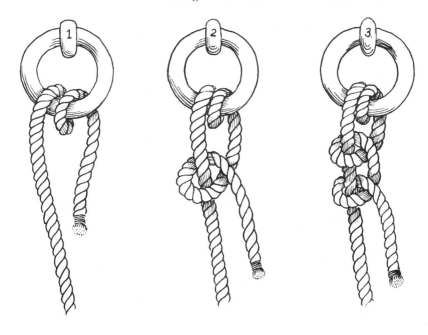

Round Turn and Two Half Hitches.

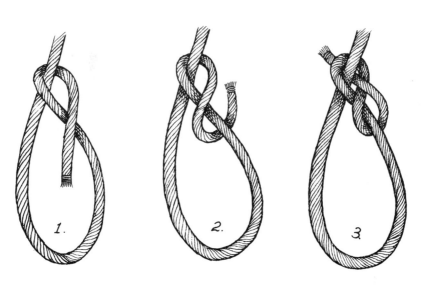

Grocer's Hitch.

is quick and easy to tie in twine or string but not very strong or reliable and not recommended for use in heavier line.

Slippery Hitch

A very useful hitch in the right circumstances. The Slippery Hitch can be released very quickly and easily. It is only safe as long as the pull on it is constant in both strength and direction and should be carefully tested before being trusted. The Slippery Hitch has proved valuable in small sailing boats, where the quick release of a line is desirable to avoid a capsize, but in modern sailing dinghies its use is obviated by the provision of jamming cleats.

Clove Hitch

A very common and widely used hitch, but not to be trusted where the direction of pull may change much, because the Clove Hitch can easily be made to slip back upon itself. Excellent for hanging things up on a rail.

Cow Hitch

As has already been mentioned, this is one way of tethering animals, but when the pull is only on one part, it is not very reliable. The Cow Hitch is better used where both ends of the rope are to be pulled, as is so in the case of the Bale Hitch. This is also a most useful hitch with any endless loop, such as an elastic band, and when used to secure the end of a line having a long eye spliced in it, will help to spread the wear upon it.

Timber Hitch

Again the name tells one what this is best used for—tying a rope around a log or logs which have to be lifted. It is a good hitch to use on anything with a fairly smooth cylindrical surface, like a broom handle, rod or pipe. Remember that it is a slip knot or noose and loses its grip as soon as the pull upon it is released.

Rolling Hitch

This is a most valuable hitch, because it can be used where all other hitches would be useless and it will never jam, but the pull on it should be from a fairly constant direction. It is the only hitch that can be relied upon to grip on a smooth surface that might roll. It is often used to take the strain off a large rope temporarily with one or more smaller ropes, whilst the end of the larger rope is made fast. The smaller ropes are hitched to the bight of the larger one by Rolling Hitches and the strain taken with them, thus leaving the end of the larger rope free to be passed around bitts or a bollard and thus secured.

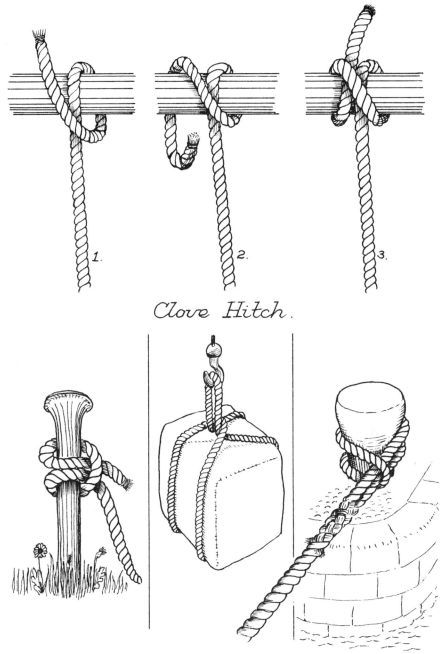

Clove Hitch.

Cow Hitch and variations.

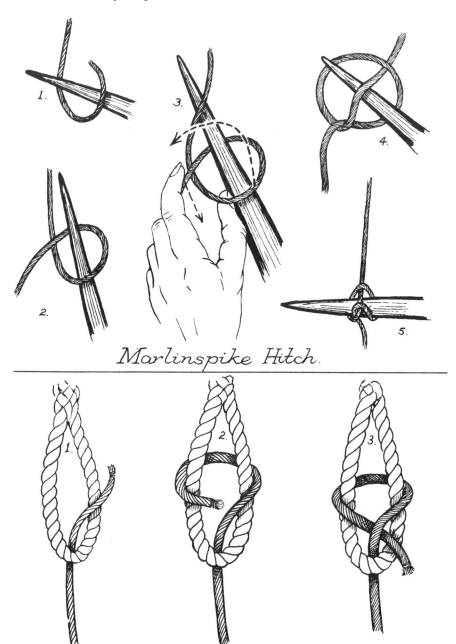

Marlinspike Hitch.

Sheet Bend.

Marlinspike Hitch

This was used by sailors and riggers to help them grip thin line, called marline, and pull it really tight when making a whipping or binding. As soon as the spike or bar is removed, the Hitch disappears. The Marlinspike Hitch can be used to pull in only one direction, as illustrated.

Sheet Bend

This is probably the best Bend of all, particularly for linking the ends of two ropes of different sizes. The Sheet Bend is one knot used in netting, but it is invariably used aboard ships for attaching a heaving line to a hawser.

Double Sheet Bend

This improves the Sheet Bend, making it more secure and ensuring that it cannot jam. It is good practice always to double a Sheet Bend if there is time in which to do so, particularly if you want to be able to rely upon it for a lengthy period of time. A Sheet Bend can be made to slip, but a Double Sheet Bend never will.

Reef Knot

Always remember that this is a Knot, it is not truly a Bend, although very often misused as one. A Reef Knot, sometimes known also as a Square Knot, should NEVER be used to tie the ends of two dissimilar lines together because it will very easily 'spill'. Prove this for yourself by tying two ends of line together with a Reef Knot and then rolling one of the loops of the knot back upon itself. You will find that it quickly spills and becomes a Cow Hitch loosely tied around the end of the other line, which can easily slip straight through it. The Reef Knot is really intended to tie the two ends of the same line together, so as to make a complete ring around a parcel or roll of something pressing uniformly outwards, as does the roll of canvas at the foot of a reefed sail. A Reef Knot Bow, which is a Reef Knot with the ends tucked back on themselves, is the way in which to tie shoe laces and bow ties, and the knot is really fit for very little else. The best rule is never to use a Reef Knot if you want to rely upon it, because it is not to be trusted. The heavier the line in which it is tied, the more likely it is that the knot will spill.

Sheepshank

A useful and reliable way in which to take up unwanted slack in a line without having to touch the ends.

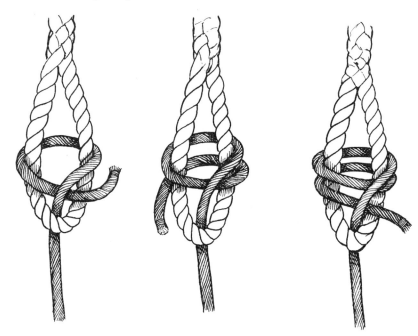

Double Sheet Bend.

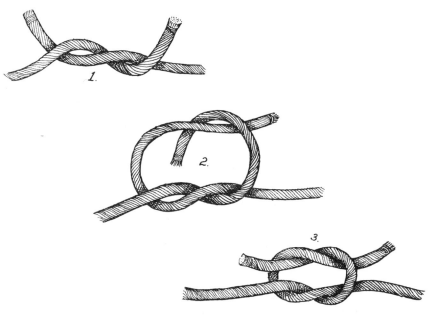

Reef Knot.

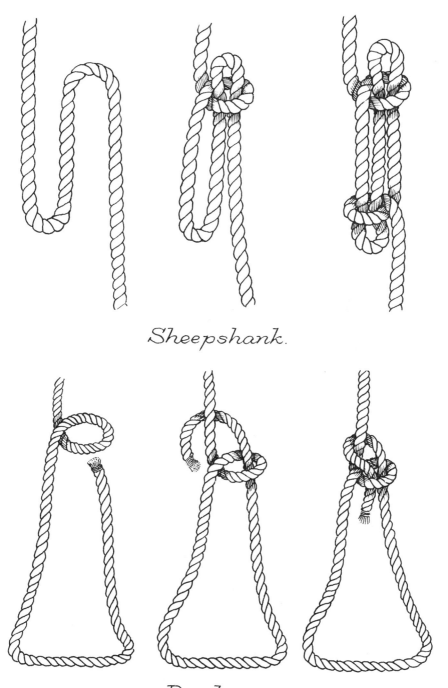

Sheepshank.

Bowline.

Bowline

This is by far the best way of making a temporary loop or eye in the end of a rope. It is very strong, reliable and will not jam however hard it is pulled upon, even when wet.

Hangman's Knot

A heavy sliding knot, designed for a single purpose, but it can be used conveniently sometimes to provide a decorative eye in a lanyard in place of an eye splice.

A Grommet

This is the correct way to make a quoit and is useful as a basis for several projects; for instance a Grommet may be covered with grafting, needle-hitching, cross-pointing, or a combination of all three, to make an attractive arm bangle. Usually Grommets are made by unlaying a piece of line of the required thickness to a distance at least four times the required circumference of the finished Grommet. Each separate strand may then be laid up again around itself, as illustrated, into a separate Grommet.

Carrick Bend

This is a strong, reliable and versatile bend, provided that it is properly made; it is in that proviso that the knot's only major fault lies, although it is also a little bulky. It is all too easy to produce a knot which looks similar in the tying, but is, in fact, unreliable and dangerous. When the Carrick Bend has been tied properly, it slips into a different form as a pull is applied to the ropes which it joins. In tying the bend an allowance for this slip should be made, by leaving the ends rather longer than would be normal for other knots. It is the above-mentioned preliminary slip in the Carrick Bend, by which its strongest form is produced from the form that is tied, that has tended to make it unpopular, and some modern authorities have ignored it completely as a bend, citing it only as the start of a number of fancy knots and mats (which this book deals with later). It is commonly stated, also, that the two ends should be seized to the standing parts after the knot has been tied. This instruction betrays a basic misunderstanding of the Carrick Bend, because, by seizing the ends back to the standing part, at any rate until after the tension has been applied and the preliminary slip has occurred, the knot is preserved in the form in which it is tied, and the slip which allows the Carrick Bend to assume its strongest form is either prevented or at least delayed. Two major advantages of the Carrick Bend are that it can be used easily and safely in really large rope, and even after very considerable tension has been applied it is relatively easy to untie and does not become jammed.

1.

2.

Hangman's Knot.

length = 4 x circumference

A Grommet.

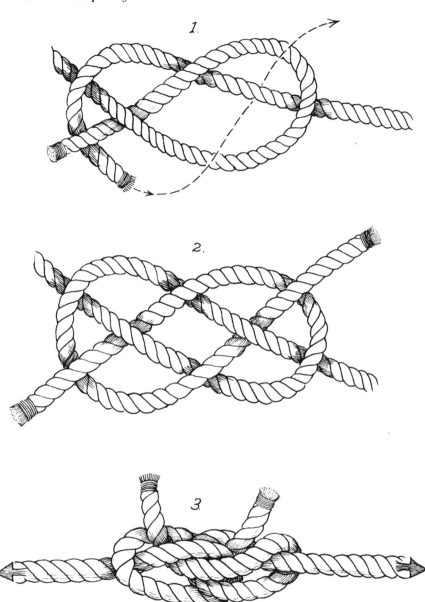

1.

2.

3.

slipped and holding in tension.

Carrick Bend.

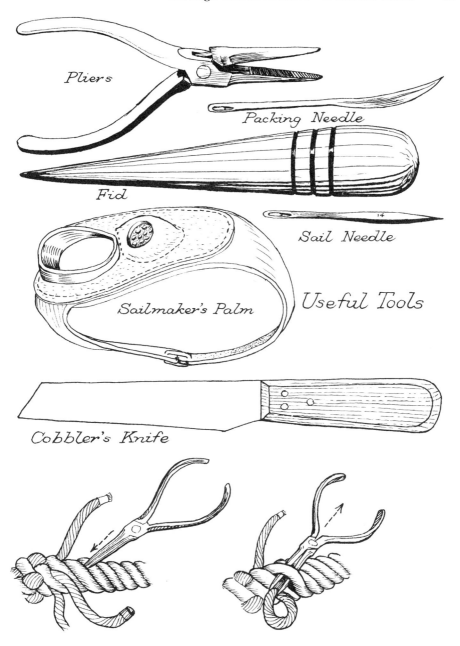

Pliers

Packing Needle

Fid

Sail Needle

Sailmaker's Palm

Useful Tools

Cobbler's Knife

Using pliers to tuck a strand in a splice.

TOOLS

Much ropecraft can be completed quite satisfactorily without using any tools except the fingers. However, for some of the more complicated multi-strand knots, particularly in small material, it will be found easier to complete the work using a pair of pliers with a fairly long, thin and pointed nose. The technique is to enter the point of the pliers from the opposite direction to that in which the strand is to lead, open the pliers enough to grasp the leading end of the strand firmly and pull it through. Preferably the holding faces of the pliers should be scored or grooved to improve their grip. If you can find the right kind of pliers, very few other tools will be found necessary, as the nose of the pliers when closed can be used as a spike. Even if you cannot buy pliers of precisely the right shape, it is not difficult to find a pair that can be modified on a grindstone to suit your own particular preferences. If you are using a wide range of material sizes, you may find it useful to have two pairs of pliers, one large and one small.

The only really essential tool is a good sharp knife. For small material up to about a centimetre in diameter, a strong modeller's knife is probably the best type to use, because sharpness is very important and sharp replacement blades are better than a blade that has been inexpertly sharpened. For larger material a cobbler's knife is probably best, being inexpensive and easy to keep sharp on a steel. Never leave the cutting edge of a knife unprotected when it is not in use, or it will become blunt very quickly. Use a strong cardboard tube or a piece of wood with a slot sawn in it as a scabbard for your knife and you will keep it sharp as well as avoiding accidental cuts.

Other tools which may be found useful include a steel spike, a hardwood spike (known as a fid), perhaps in two or three sizes, a hardwood mallet, sail needles size fourteen up to size ten (the lower the number the larger the size), two or three packing needles of a similar size range, and a sailmaker's palm.

2 Bindings, multi-strand knots and splices

Before attempting to tie multi-strand knots, the strands must be secured together. A piece of self-adhesive tape may do perfectly well where it will not be seen after the work is completed, and ordinary masking tape is quite strong enough to prevent ends from fraying out in most materials. Where a more permanent and finished appearance is required, a proper whipping is essential, and where strength of grip is needed a binding knot might be best.

Common Whipping
This is the whipping most commonly used to bind the end of a rope neatly.

Sailmaker's Whipping
A better looking and more secure whipping in which, after binding around the lay of the rope, the twine is passed between two strands above the binding, down parallel with the lay across the binding, through the strands below the binding, back up across the binding parallel with the lay, between two strands again, and so on all the way around, finishing off with the end of the twine buried between the strands below the whipping.

Palm and Needle Whipping
Very similar in appearance to the Sailmaker's Whipping, the only difference being that, as the name implies, a needle is used to stitch the twine between the strands instead of simply tucking it by hand.

27

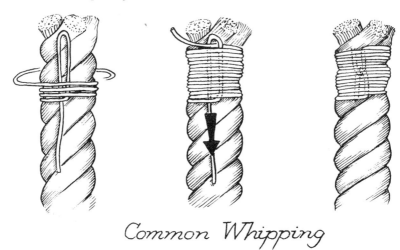

Common Whipping

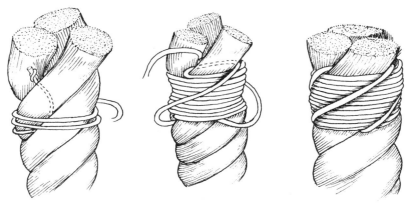

Sailmaker's Whipping.

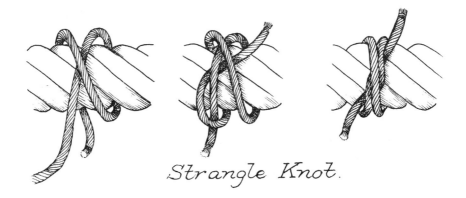

Strangle Knot.

Strangle Knot
This is a quick and neat way of binding several strands together, without the labour of making a whipping. The Strangle Knot is better looking than the Constrictor Knot, but is rather less secure, particularly on an uneven surface. The Strangle Knot and Constrictor Knot depend for their secure holding power upon the over-riding turn, which makes them very difficult to untie.

Double Turn Strangle Knot
This improves both the security and the appearance of the simple Strangle Knot. It is very difficult to untie, once hauled tight, and may have to be cut if removal is necessary.

Constrictor Knot
An invaluable binding knot for securing several strands together. It is better than the Strangle Knot when applied to an uneven surface, although rather more bulky in appearance. Note that both the Constrictor and Strangle Knots consist of an Overhand Knot with an over-riding turn applied; the difference between the two knots lies solely in the direction in which the over-riding turn crosses the overhand knot below it. This difference is small but subtle and important, so it is worth taking a little trouble to understand it.

Double Turn Constrictor Knot
The extra over-riding turn improves the appearance of the Constrictor Knot and makes it almost impossible to untie once it has been pulled up tight.

Extra over-riding turns may easily be added to both Constrictor and Strangle Knots, and Triple or Quadruple Turn Knots provide simple and secure whippings, for the ends can be trimmed off close to the knot without detriment to its security once it has been hauled tight. Some books illustrate these knots used as tourniquets to prevent bleeding from a badly cut limb, but it is *extremely dangerous* to apply either of these knots to the human body in any way, because they are so very difficult to release, and, being very efficient bindings, will quickly cut off the circulation. To learn about tourniquets it would be better to study a book about First Aid rather than one about knots.

Crown Knot
This is probably the easiest multi-strand knot. It is illustrated here, as are the other knots in this chapter, tied in a three strand rope, but this does not mean that these knots can only be tied with three strands. On the contrary, there is

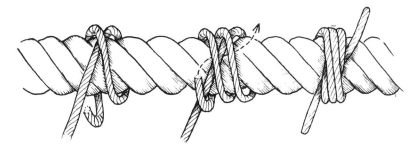

Double Turn Strangle Knot.

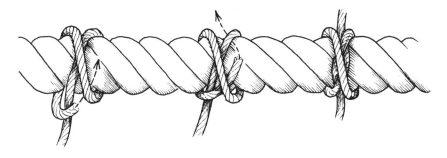

Constrictor Knot.

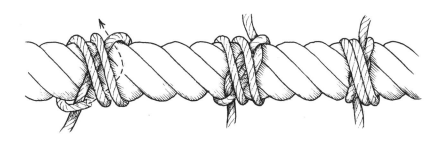

Double Turn Constrictor Knot.

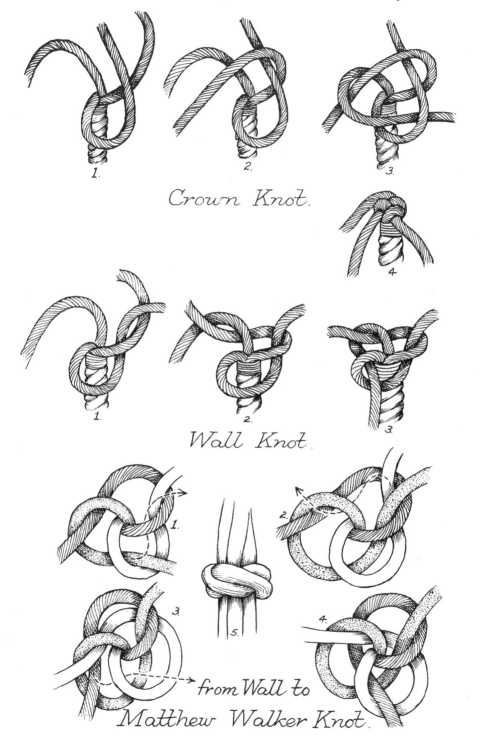

Crown Knot.

Wall Knot.

from Wall to
Matthew Walker Knot.

no theoretical limit to the number of strands used, although above five strands will usually need to be tied around a core. A series of Crown Knots produces a handsome form of plait or sennit.

Wall Knot
Another simple multi-strand knot, here illustrated tied in three strands for easy understanding. Neither the Wall Knot nor the preceding Crown are often used by themselves, but they are very important, and should be practised until really familiar, because they are the basis upon which many other multi-strand knots are built and if they are clearly understood, other more complicated knots will be found relatively easy.

Matthew Walker Knot
This knot appears at first glance to be much more complicated than it really is, so refuse to panic, and note that it is really quite simply derived from the Wall Knot which precedes it. First tie a Wall Knot as above, fairly loosely, then take one strand and pass it up through the next loop to the right, alongside the second strand. Now take the second strand and tuck it up alongside the third strand. Finally take the third strand and push it up into the space originally occupied by the first strand. After pulling each strand tight, it may be found that rolling the whole knot towards the open end of the line will help to form it properly.

Double Matthew Walker Knot
By following exactly the same procedure which converted the Wall into the Matthew Walker Knot, the Matthew Walker can be converted into the Double Matthew Walker Knot. Thus, if one can tie a Wall Knot, there is no reason why one should not be able to achieve a single or double Matthew Walker Knot, yet these are often regarded as fiendishly difficult, and only to be attempted by the expert. The reason is probably that to tie these knots without going through the intermediate stages does require a degree of expertise, but it is surely the result rather than the method which is important. It is also worth bearing in mind that, when numerous strands are being used, it is often better to work through the intermediate stages, because this keeps the design even throughout and avoids any possibility of a mistake. When working with twenty or thirty strands, a mistake can be infuriatingly laborious to correct!

Footrope Knot
'Make a Crown and then a Wall, tuck the ends up and that's all.' The Foot-rope Knot was used in the footropes, which ran along below the yards of a

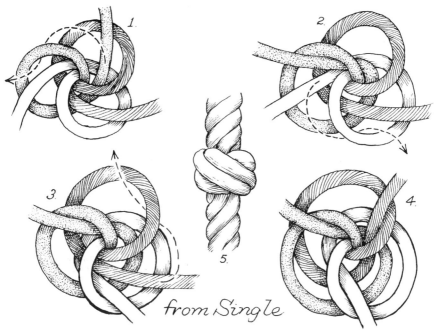

from Single

to Double Matthew Walker Knot.

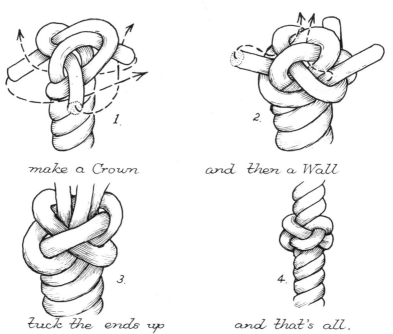

make a Crown   *and then a Wall*

tuck the ends up   *and that's all.*

Footrope Knot.

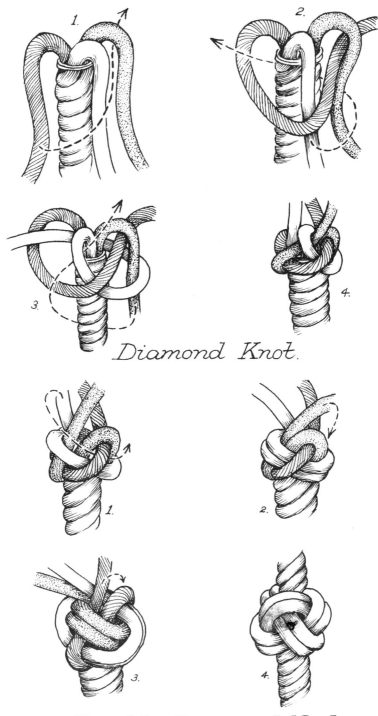

Diamond Knot.

Double Diamond Knot.

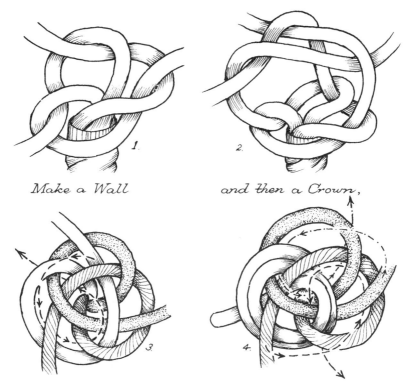

Make a Wall   and then a Crown,

double the lead   and tuck the ends down.

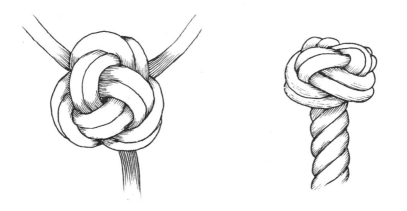

Manrope Knot.

square-rigged sailing ship and which the sailors stood upon while handling the sails aloft. The knots provided a better grip for the feet. The Footrope Knot closely resembles the Diamond Knot, but the Footrope Knot is the more stable.

Diamond Knot

In its simple form the Diamond Knot is not often used, the Footrope Knot being preferable. However, the Diamond is easier to double, as follows, and to extend, as is shown later.

Double Diamond Knot

This is the form of Diamond Knot normally used. The illustration shows the knot being doubled by following each strand above the lead of the original knot, which is usual, and allows the strands to be laid up again in the normal way after completing the knot. If the Diamond Knot is used as a terminal knot, it may be doubled by following below the lead of the original knot and cutting the ends off close, or, perhaps better, finish by tripling the first part of the knot (following around for a third time) and cutting the ends off close under the completed knot.

Manrope Knot

'Make a Wall and then a Crown, double the lead and tuck the ends down.' The Manrope knot is simply a doubled Wall and Crown, with the lead being followed above the original strand and the ends being finally tucked down through the centre of the knot before tightening. If the lead is followed below the original strand, as it can be, the final knot has a squarer appearance.

SPLICES

All the illustrations show splices made in three strand right hand laid rope, because this is by far the most common type of rope. In the unlikely event that other types of laid rope are encountered, the principles indicated below can be applied. Note particularly that in all except Long Splices the strands being spliced are tucked 'against the lay', so that with a right hand laid rope, the strands of which normally spiral away from the observer in a clockwise direction, the strands of the splice spiral away anti-clockwise.

Back Splice

This is a useful way of preventing the ends of a line from fraying out, particularly in small line which cannot be whipped, or when suitable whipping

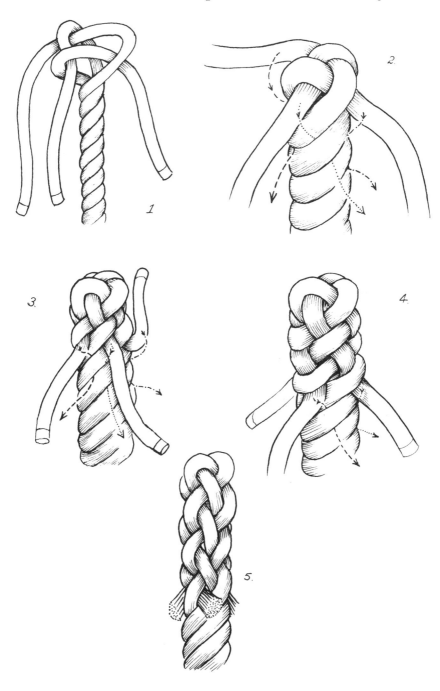

Back Splice.

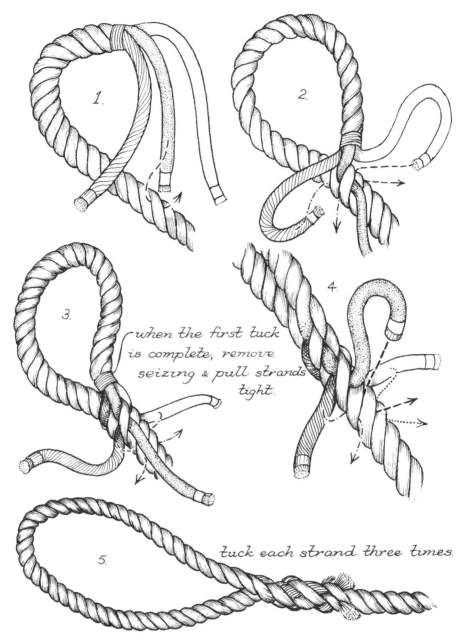

1.

2.

3.

when the first tuck
is complete, remove
seizing & pull strands
tight.

4.

5.

tuck each strand three times.

Eye Splice.

material is not available. This is probably the easiest splice to learn and practice, and, as the principle is the same as that of the more important eye splice and short splice, it is explained first. When worked in small material, which is the only proper place for a back splice, it will not be necessary for the ends of the strands to be whipped, but it may be found helpful to dip the ends in a quick-drying glue so that they will not fray out for the purposes of learning and practising. Unlay the strands of the line for a distance of about five or six times the circumference of the line and make a Crown Knot with the three strands. Next pass each strand in turn *against the lay* over one laid strand and tuck it under the next. After each strand has been tucked once, they should emerge equally spaced around the circumference of the line, with a laid strand separating each of the unlaid strands one from another. Each working strand in turn is again passed against the lay over one and under the next laid strand for a second and then a third time and after each tuck the three strands should emerge equidistant around the circumference of the line. If they do not, then a mistake has been made, which must be corrected before proceeding. After the third tuck has been completed satisfactorily, cut the ends of the working strands off, leaving a small tuft of each, then roll the whole splice between the palms of the hands to make it as neat and even as possible.

Eye Splice

Whip or tape around the ends of the strands and similarly seize (whip or tape) around the whole rope at a distance of roughly five times the rope's circumference from the end. This is only an approximate guide and always err on the generous side, which will allow you plenty of material to work with. Unlay the strands as far as the seizing and fold the rope over to form an eye of the desired size, laying the seizing against the rope at the point where the splice is to begin. Take the unlaid strand which emerges from the seizing farthest away from the rope and tuck it beneath the laid strand closest to the seizing. The two remaining unlaid strands should fall one on each side of the tucked strand, and should themselves be tucked beneath the two laid strands which lie on each side of the first tucked strand. At this stage the three tucked unlaid strands should emerge equally spaced around the circumference of the rope, with a laid strand separating each from the others, as diagram 3 in this sequence illustrates. The seizing can be removed now and each strand pulled snug, but not so tight as to distort any part of the rope. Each of the unlaid strands in turn is now passed over one laid strand *against the lay* and tucked beneath the next. After completing the second set of tucks the splice should appear as in diagram 4 of the sequence, again with the working strands

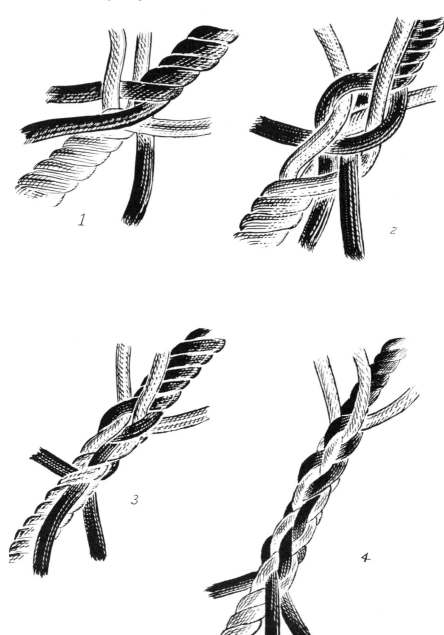

Short Splice.

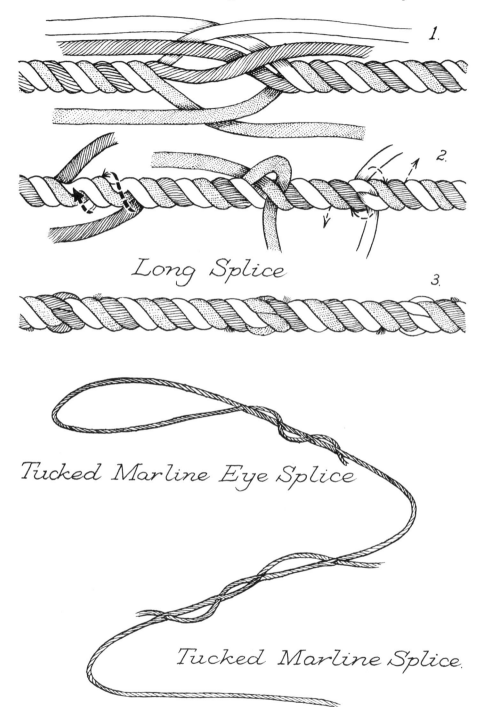

1.

2.

Long Splice

3.

Tucked Marline Eye Splice

Tucked Marline Splice

emerging equidistant around the rope's circumference. Take each strand once more one and under the next laid strand as before, so that each strand should have been tucked three times in all, emerging once again equally spaced around the rope's circumference. After pulling each strand tight and neat, cut the end off, leaving a small tuft. Do not cut the ends off too close to the rope, or the last tuck may not hold and the splice may gradually work loose. Three tucks are normally adequate to prevent an eye splice from slipping, but in large ropes sometimes the working strands may be divided after the final tuck, half of each strand then being seized to half of each of its neighbours. For better appearance and hard wearing, a third of the emerging yarns may be cut out from each working strand after the third tuck; a fourth tuck is then made and a further third of the yarns removed before making the fifth and final tuck. This tapers the splice, which may then be 'served', that is bound tightly around and covered by repeated turns of twine.

Short Splice
This is the quickest and most often used means of permanently joining the two ends of a line or joining together two pieces of the same kind of rope. It is strong, but a length of rope with a splice in it is never as strong as the rope itself. Unlay the strands of the two ends to be joined, to a distance of about four or five times the rope's circumference, and whip the ends of the strands. Place the two ends together with the strands alternating, as shown in diagram 1 of this sequence. This is called 'marrying' the ends. At this stage you may find it helpful to seize one set of strands to the opposing rope and commence work with the other set of strands exclusively. Having completed two tucks with one set of strands, the seizing can be released and the other set of strands tucked twice in its turn. It is usual to tuck the two sets of strands alternately, but, providing the completed splice is even, and each set of strands is tucked twice beyond the marrying point, the sequence of working is not important. The strands are tucked as in the eye splice and back splice, against the lay, over one strand and under the next alternately. The ends of the strands are normally cut off, leaving a small tuft, but the splice may sometimes be tapered and served over as described for the eye splice.

Long Splice
This type of splice, and there are many variations of it, is used when the spliced rope has to pass through a pulley block, or when appearance is important and the splice must be unobtrusive. Note that much more rope has to be used in making a long splice than in making a short splice. The proportions of the long splice are approximately to scale in the illustration.

One strand of each rope is unlaid a little more than the full length of the splice, and the other two strands of each rope are unlaid for a little more than half the length of the splice. At the centre point of the splice one of the half unlaid strands from each rope is joined to the other by a simple overhand knot. The other two half unlaid strands are then laid up on the opposite rope in the places of the two fully unlaid strands. When the opposing strands meet at each end of the splice, they are joined by an overhand knot. The ends of the strands protruding from the three overhand knots are then tucked once, against the lay, to each side of the knots. They are either cut off at this point, or may be halved and tucked again before being trimmed off.

Tucked Marline Eye Splice
Often used at the commencement of half-hitching (described in detail later), where a running eye in small material is required, without a bulky knot spoiling the appearance. This can be useful also for eye splices in the rigging of model ships. The end of the length of twine is tucked back through its own lay four times.

Tucked Marline Splice
This is a useful and quite adequately strong means of joining two lengths of small material without using a bulky and obvious knot, which would spoil the continuity and appearance of decorative work. The two ends are merely tucked twice through the lay of the other.

3 Single strand fancy knots

Probably the most important single strand fancy knots are those known as 'Turk's Heads'. The name undoubtedly arises from the similarity between these knots and a turban. I only use the name for the very wide range of single strand multi-lead knots, of which only a very few basic ones are described here. A book of respectable size could be written on this single subject, but the practical value of large single strand knots is doubtful. When the number of leads in a Turk's Head exceeds four or five, and the leads are doubled or tripled, the knot becomes wider than its tubular diameter, unless the number of bights is large. To produce a tubular covering knot of such a shape it is easier and quicker to make a similar knot, which can be of identical appearance, using several strands together. Such multi-strand knots are described in a later chapter; however I do not call them Turk's Heads, although the term is often used to include multi-strand tubular knots.

Turk's Heads are usually tied over a hard core, such as a rod or tube, and they were often used to decorate telescopes, knives and hand rails, also the midships spoke of a ship's wheel usually carries a Turk's Head to identify it in the dark. If the material used for tying the knot is sufficiently stiff to hold its shape, it can be made to stand on its own. For instance leather bootlaces are used to tie small scarf rings worn by Boy Scouts, and the coloured polypropylene lines, cane or even plastic-covered wire may be used to make table-napkin rings or bracelets. The main problem always is to secure the ends effectively but unobtrusively. With rope this is fairly easily done by careful stitching, leather may also be stitched or glued, but other materials require special techniques; for instance many plastics can be heat-welded by the careful application of a hot soldering iron.

Three Lead Four Bight Turk's Head

Three lead Turk's Heads are identical to a simple three strand plait, but made in an endless loop with only a single strand. The single strand passes around the knot once per lead, which is usually either doubled or tripled, so in a three lead Turk's Head which is tripled, the single strand makes nine complete circuits around the circumference of whatever the knot is being tied around.

In deciding how much rope is needed to make a Turk's Head, take the number of leads, plus one extra to allow for the weave of the knot, and multiply this by the number of times the lead is to be followed, then multiply that product by the circumference of the core to be covered. For example, suppose that we wish to tie a three lead tripled Turk's Head around a telescope, of which the surface circumference is six inches:

$$(3 \text{ leads} + 1 = 4) \times 3 \times 6 \text{ inches} = 72 \text{ inches or six feet}$$

In practice—and I have tested this formula many times—this allows almost exactly the right amount of line needed for the average Turk's Head, but if many bights are intended or the line being used is of a large size, allow extra. In any case it is always as well to err on the generous side, because there is nothing more frustrating than to lavish time and concentration on producing a beautifully made knot, only to find that six inches more line than one has allowed is needed to complete the masterpiece!

The start shown in diagrams 1, 2 and 3 of this sequence produces a four bight Turk's Head, which is the easiest to produce. The number of bights can be extended by three extra simply by an additional transposition of the two initial leads, as shown in diagram 2 of the sequence, followed by passing the third lead over the second and under the first. Note the rule that the second lead (or turn) always passes over the first, and the third lead always passes over the second and under the first. By this means the number of bights may be increased, always by three at a time, as often as is convenient to suit a particular circumference.

After completing the knot (the point at which the two ends meet in opposite directions) the lead is followed all the way around the knot until it has been doubled. This process may be repeated to triple or even quadruple the lead. Either end or both ends together may be used in the process of doubling the lead and it is often convenient to commence tying the knot at the centre of the length of line being used, thus having two ends of moderate length to use in doubling the lead from two directions, rather than a single end of excessive

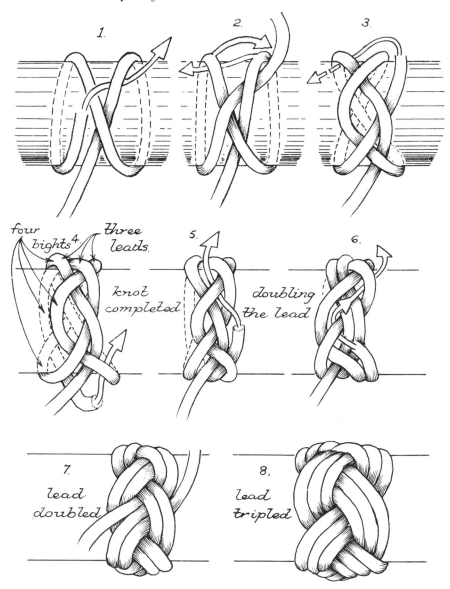

four bights   three leads.

knot completed

doubling the lead

lead doubled

lead tripled

Three Lead Four Bight Turk's Head

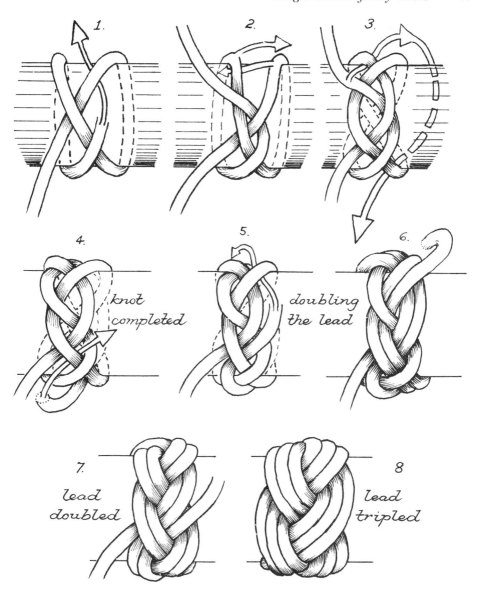

1.

2.

3.

4.

knot completed

5.

doubling the lead

6.

7.

lead doubled

8

lead tripled

Three Lead Five Bight Turk's Head.

length, all of which has to be pulled through at each tuck.

When the whole knot has been tied, work it tight by pulling up any slack through successive bights right out to the ends. A pair of pointed pliers is most useful for this, but a small spike also may be found helpful. Finally, when the whole knot is firm and even, cut off the ends as close to the knot as possible. The cut ends should not be visible after completing a well-tied knot.

Three Lead Five Bight Turk's Head

This start provides a two bight Turk's Head, to which three further bights are added each time the two initial leads are transposed and interwoven by the third lead. Look carefully at diagram 1 of this sequence. If the end of the line, from which the arrow extends, is passed directly around behind the core and up to join the other end, a three lead two bight Turk's Head is formed. By exchanging the positions of two bights as shown in diagram 2 and continuing the third lead through them, as shown in diagrams 3 and 4, three more bights are formed on each side of the completed knot. If the diameter of the rod or tube to be covered is large, still more bights can be formed in the knot by again exchanging the positions of a bight from each side of the knot, as in diagram 2, and every additional exchange adds three more bights to the completed knot. Finish by working the knot snug and cutting off the ends close as described above.

Four Lead Three Bight Turk's Head

Notice that this start consists of a simple overhand knot and the rest of the knot is produced by following one fundamental rule, which is that each successive lead is placed ahead of the one which immediately precedes it and is tucked in the opposite sense to its predecessor. That is to say where the preceding lead is tucked over and under, the following lead is tucked under and over. If this rule is followed, Turk's Heads from either of the two starts shown here for the three lead five bight Turk's Head and for the four lead three bight Turk's Head can be raised by two leads and two bights, thus the reader can produce five and six lead Turk's Heads, which is as far as this book will go into this particular subject.

Flat Turk's Heads

It is a useful function of the Turk's Head that the same knot can be made both tubular, as has been shown already, and flat, as these illustrations show. In their flat form Turk's Heads can be used to make basically circular mats. It is not possible to bury the ends but they should be kept to the underside of the mat and are usually secured in place by stitching them to their neighbouring

distribute the bights
evenly around the
circumference and
double the lead.

Four Lead Three Bight Turk's Head.

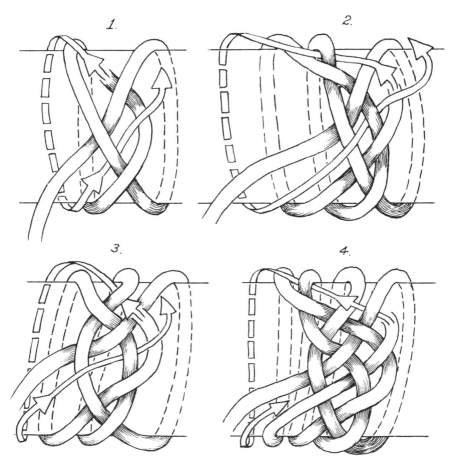

distribute the bights evenly around the circumference,
and double the lead.

Five Lead Four Bight Turk's Head.

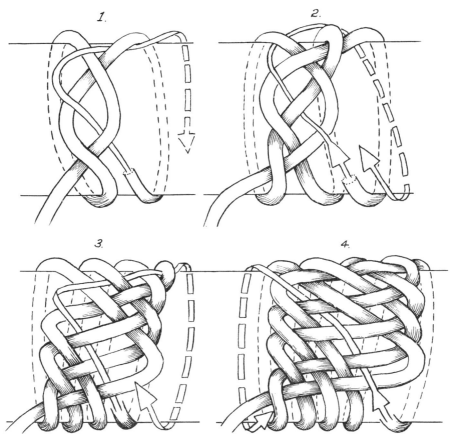

distribute the bights evenly and double the lead.

Six Lead Five Bight Turk's Head.

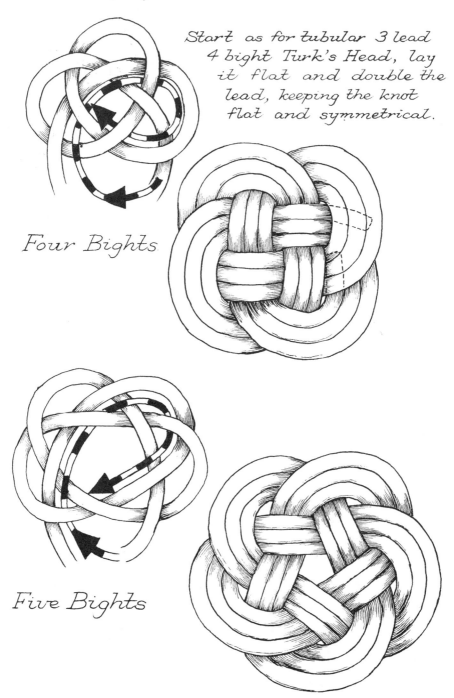

Start as for tubular 3 lead
4 bight Turk's Head, lay
it flat and double the
lead, keeping the knot
flat and symmetrical.

Four Bights

Five Bights

Flat Turk's Heads, 3 Leads.

parallel leads and to the bight lying above. The two Turk's Heads illustrated are three lead, four and five bights, and these simple knots are probably the best suited to the flat form. The larger the number of bights used, the larger the hole in the middle of the mat becomes; this fact can be utilized in making a circular mat, by placing a simple Turk's Head of few bights inside one of a larger number of bights. For instance the three lead four bight Turk's Head will fit neatly into the space in the centre of a three lead eight bight Turk's Head. Notice that the start is exactly the same, whether the knot is to be tubular or flat.

Prolong Knot

This is really a method of extending a flat three lead four bight Turk's Head into a rectangular form. The start is precisely the same as that which has already been shown for the three lead four bight Turk's Head, but the method of tying it as a Prolong Knot is slightly different, principally because it is convenient to hang the knot on a hook or nail for working. Having tied the start, the two bights through which the ends pass are lengthened, twisted through half a turn in the same direction, and one placed across the other as illustrated in diagram 2 of the sequence. The two ends are then woven through the extended loops as shown in diagram 3 of the sequence. If one extension is sufficient, the ends are turned in towards each other to complete the knot and proceed with doubling the lead. The knot may be extended further, however, and to a degree only limited by the amount of line available, by lengthening the two loops again and repeating the interweaving procedure as shown in diagrams 2 and 3.

Ocean Plait

A very similar technique to the Prolong Knot, whereby a simple overhand knot is extended as often as required and then doubled. Whereas the first extension of the Prolong Knot produces four bights per side, the Ocean Plait's first extension produces three bights per side. Each additional extension of either the Ocean Plait or the Prolong Knot provides a further three bights per side; the extension technique remains the same throughout.

Carrick Bend Mats

The Carrick Bend is fully described in Chapter 1 where its advantages and disadvantages as a bend are detailed. It is not a single strand knot in the true sense, although it may be tied in the two ends of a single strand, so it does not strictly belong in this chapter. The mats which can be developed from the Carrick Bend, however, bear a very close resemblance to those immediately

1.

2.

3.

Single extension,
   doubled lead.

Prolong Knot.

1.

2.

3.

4.

1st. extension

2nd. extension.

5.

lead doubled.

Ocean Plait.

1.

Carrick Bend.

2.

1st. extension.

3a.

doubling the lead.

4a.

3b.

2nd extension.

4b.

Carrick Bend Mats.

preceding, therefore it is convenient to consider them in the same category.

When making this type of mat, it is usual to make the Carrick Bend in the centre of two lines of equal length, thus one has four ends of equal length with which to work. The procedure of doubling the lead after the first extension, shown in diagrams 3a and 4a of the sequence, produces a mat almost identical in appearance to the product of a single extension, doubled lead Ocean Plait, but with four ends to be hidden instead of two. For this reason the Ocean Plait version of the design is usually preferable. The procedure of further extending the Carrick Bend, retaining the single lead and allowing the four ends to protrude from the corners, as shown in diagrams 3b and 4b, can be used to produce a rectangular mat of any convenient size. Regardless of the number of extensions, one pair of sides will always have one more bight than the other, each extension adding one more bight to each side. The ends may be tucked under the edge and secured by stitching, but they may be conveniently formed into tassels. A simple way of doing this, when the line is formed of laid strands, is to tie the strands in a single or double Matthew Walker knot or a double Diamond knot and, when the knot is tight, comb the protruding yarns out evenly and trim them off at an equal length.

The Monkey's Fist
This is used at sea still for providing a weighted knot in the leading end of a heaving line. For this purpose the Monkey's Fist is tied, but not tightened, and then a small heavy object, such as a steel or brass nut or a large ball-bearing, is placed inside as a core. The knot is worked tight over the core, and the short end of the line is often spliced back into the long remainder. The Monkey's Fist can be tied in a variety of ways, using a single end or both ends, but it normally requires a core of some description to be inserted before working tight. A rough ball of rag, paper or cotton waste is adequate if no weight is required. For decorative purposes, or where the Monkey's Fist is made to use as a ball, for which purpose it serves admirably, either or both of the ends may be cut off close once the knot has been worked tight. The tying method illustrated here is probably the quickest and is easy to remember, but, once the principle of the knot is understood, it is not difficult to develop variations on the theme. The illustrated sequence shows the knot being tied having three turns in each dimension, which is most common; but there is no reason why the number of turns in each dimension should not be increased or decreased if it is convenient to do so.

The Drummer Boy's Plait
A single strand sennit, this, named for its use on old-fashioned drums for

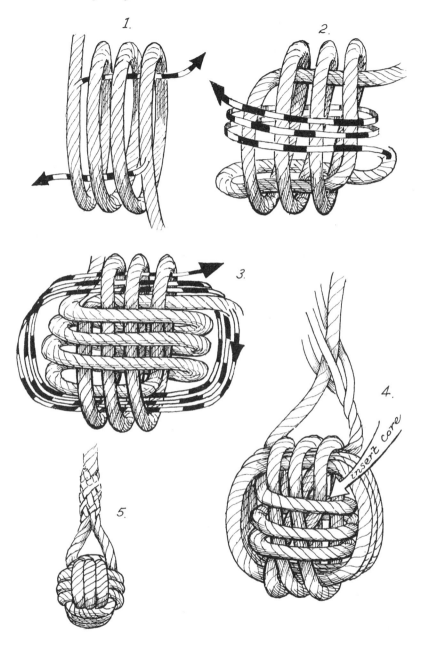

Monkey's Fist.

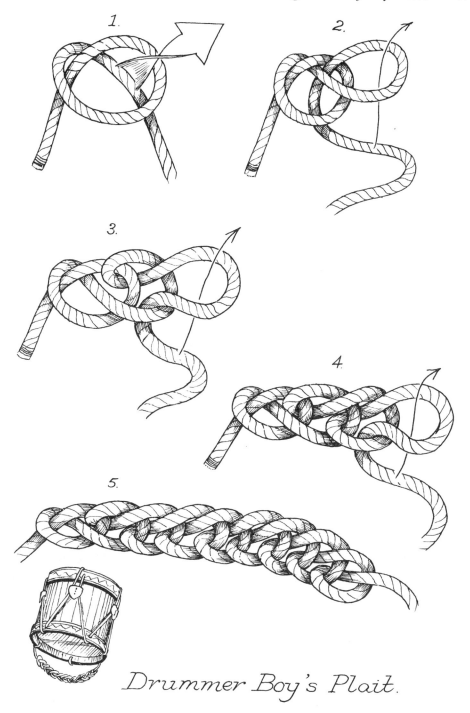

1.

2.

3.

4.

5.

Drummer Boy's Plait.

taking up the remaining line after the drum cord had been threaded and tightened. A considerable additional length of spare cord could be carried conveniently and decoratively in this way during a campaign. Modern military drums have metal screw fittings instead of cords, but the decorative 'drag cords' are often still carried. The Drummer Boy's Plait is a useful way of keeping spare line in full view and immediately available. By withdrawing the end from the final bight, a convenient amount of line may be pulled out from the plait and the remainder secured as before by passing the end again through a new final bight. The length of line contained in a Drummer Boy's Plait is about five times the length of the plait itself.

4   Plaits and sennits of up to six strands

Plaits and sennits are methods of weaving or interlacing a number of strands, often of different colour and size, into a decorative band or rope of any desired length. This process is also sometimes called braiding. The terms 'plait', 'sennit' and 'braid' are, to some extent, interchangeable and can not be clearly separated. Even the normal usage and spelling of these terms varies from place to place, in different trades and even between individuals. As a rough guide one may assume that a plait is a fairly simple procedure; braid is mainly an industrial product, although the term is still sometimes applied to hair arrangement. (A schoolgirl's plaits or braids are usually in the form of a three strand plait—No. I.) The word sennit probably has the narrowest use, being uncommon in circles which do not habitually make use of this particular skill. I use the terms 'plait' and 'sennit' only in the sense and spelling that the average British seaman would understand, and I make no claims to definitive correctness.

Basically there are three kinds of sennit, differentiated by their sectional shape: flat, square and round. Flat sennits are useful for belts and straps, whereas round and square sennits are preferable for decorative handles and cords. Other sectional shapes, such as half-round, crescent and oval are possible in special sennits, but the subject is a wide one and is not dealt with in great depth in this book.

The use for which the proposed sennit is intended will probably determine how it shall be started. Four different ways of securing the strands of flat

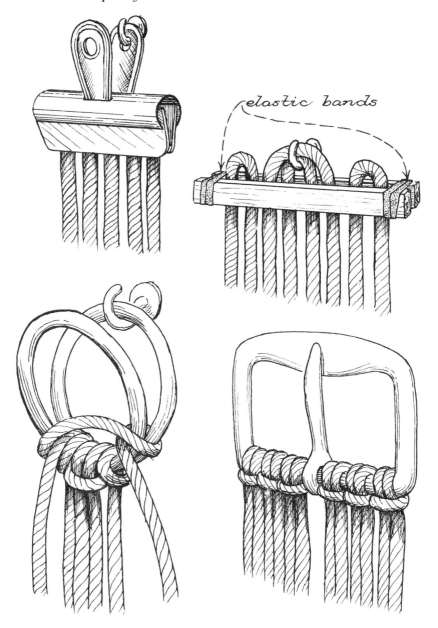

Securing the strands of a Sennit.

sennits are illustrated and a fifth possibility is to sew the ends of the strands together inside a suitable piece of leather or cloth. Round and square sennits can be started with the strands held together by a whipping.

Every sennit has a rule, by which the order and manner in which the strands are interwoven is governed. The pattern of the sennit is achieved by the continuous repetition of this rule and it is important that the repetition is evenly maintained throughout the sennit. It is not necessary to work with the strands taut, but it is essential that an even tension, however slight, be maintained, or the uniformity of the finished product may be spoiled. The rule for each sennit is stated below the relevant illustrations.

In the illustrations all the strands are shown to be of the same size, but in some sennits this may not be necessary or even desirable. Similarly it may be advantageous to use strands of different colours or texture in certain sennits. In the illustrations of some more complicated sennits some strands are shaded, but this is in order to make the drawing as clear as possible and it should not be taken as an indication that strands shown shaded in a drawing should be of a different colour in practice. In deciding which sennits provide opportunity for such variations it is helpful to examine the two pages which illustrate sixteen different completed sennits. You will notice that in No. XII the centre strand maintains a straight line throughout and therefore could be of a different colour, texture and size from the rest of the strands without any detriment to the design. In No. V two strands maintain a line down the centre of the sennit and so could be different in appearance from the other three strands, although preferably the same as each other. In Nos. IV and VIII each strand maintains its own individual line throughout, so that, theoretically, each strand could be of a different colour. In No. VIII the size of the two *pairs* of interweaving strands could be different, but the two strands in each pair must be of the same size. In No. IV the centre strand and the strand which weaves from side to side may be of different sizes from all the others, but the pair of strands running parallel with and on each side of the centre strand in the illustration should be of the same size, and, preferably, of the same colour.

Where it is possible, in a particular sennit, to use a strand of a different size from the others, it is also possible to use two or more strands as one. For instance, in No. XII the single centre strand could be replaced satisfactorily by two or three parallel strands, perhaps of a contrasting colour and size.

In some flat sennits two strands constantly cross and re-cross each other on the centre-line, passing to alternate edges of the sennit between crossings. Examples of such sennits are Nos. III, XIV, and XV. Each *pair* of strands which interchange symmetrically in such sennits may have a distinctive colour or texture, but the size of all the strands should be the same.

II.   III.   IV.   V.

VI.   VII.   VIII.   IX.

X.   XI.   XII.   XIII.

XIV.   XV.   XVI.   XVII.

I. *Three Strand Plait.*

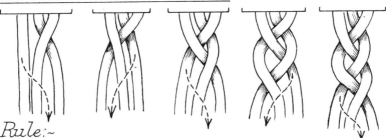

Rule:~

Outside right to centre, outside left to centre, and repeat.

II. *Five Strand Plait.*

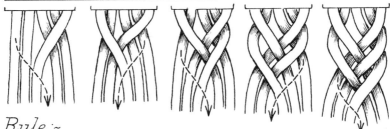

Rule:~

Outside right over two to centre, outside left over two to centre, and repeat.

III. *Four Strand French Sennit.*

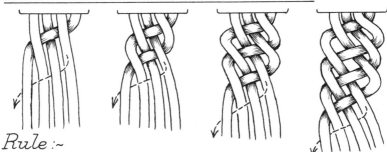

Rule:~

Outside right under one, over one alternately to left outside. This method can be used with any number of strands.

IV. Woven Plait.

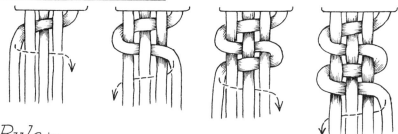

Rule:~

Outside right under and over alternately to outside left, return over & under to outside right and repeat. This method can be used with any number of strands.

V. Five Strand Flat Sennit.

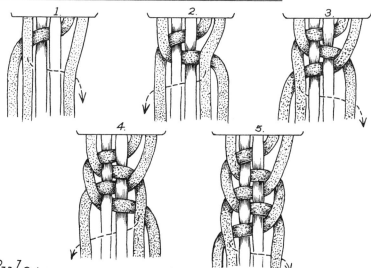

Rule:~

Second from right under & over alternately to outside left; second from left similarly to outside right and repeat.

VI. Five Strand French Sennit.

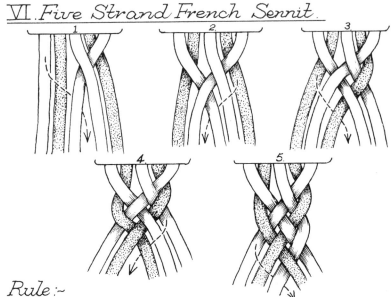

Rule:-

Outside right over and under alternately to centre, outside left similarly to centre, and repeat.

VII. Alternative Method for VI.

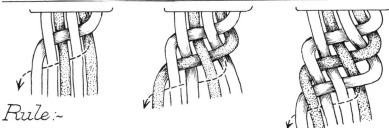

Rule:-

Outside right over & under alternately to outside left, and repeat.

Note: the construction of this sennit is identical with that of VI above although different in appearance. See Nᵒˢ III & XIV where the same alternatives may be applied.

VIII. Four Strand Square Sennit.

Rule :~

Outside left & right, passing between inner pair, exchange places; inner left & right, passing between outer pair, exchange places, and repeat, maintaining lines of exchange.

IX. Four Strand Round Sennit.

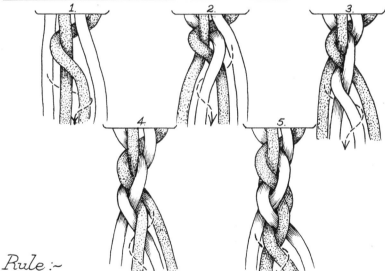

Rule :~

Outside right behind and around inner left, outside left behind and around inner right, and repeat.

X. Five Strand Square Sennit.

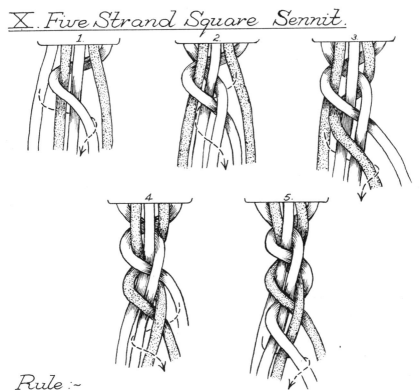

Rule :-

Outside right behind and around inner left two, outside left behind and around inner right, and repeat.

XI. Three Part Plait With Six Strands.

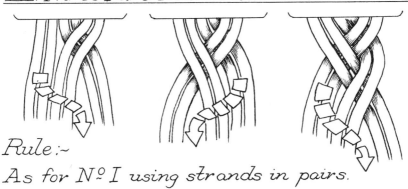

Rule :-

As for Nº I using strands in pairs.

XII. Six Strand Flat Sennits.

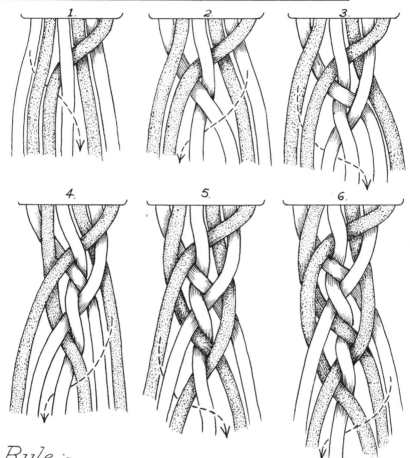

Rule :-

Outside right inward <u>over</u> two and <u>under</u> one, outside left inward <u>under</u> two and <u>over</u> one.

Note :- the strand running through the centre of this sennit, being independent, may be different in texture, size and shape from the other strands.

XIII. Six Strand Flat Sennits

Rule :-

Outside right inward over one and under one, outside left inward over one, under one and over one, and repeat.

Note :- this sennit is asymmetric and tends to curve in section while being worked, but can be made to lie flat without difficulty. If necessary hammer lightly using a wooden mallet.

XIV. Six Strand French Sennit.

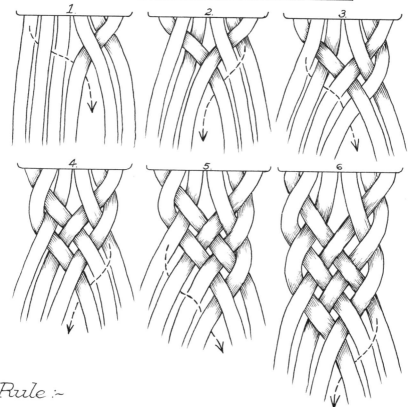

Rule :-

Outside right inward over one and under one, outside left inward under one, over one and under one, and repeat. An identically constructed sennit of different appearance may be made by taking outside right (or left) over one, under one alternately to the opposite side and repeating the process.

XV. Six Strand Flat Sennits.

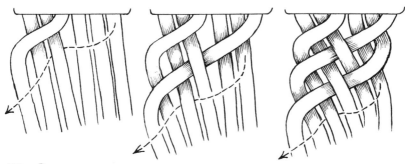

Rule :~

Third from left over two to outside left,
then, repeating, outside right over two,
under one and over two to outside left.

XVI. Six Strand Square Sennit.

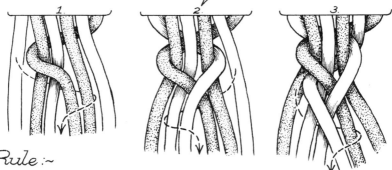

Rule :~

Outside right to left behind four and
to centre in front of two, outside left
to right behind four and to centre in
front of two, and repeat.

Diagrams continue on next page.

XVI *continued*

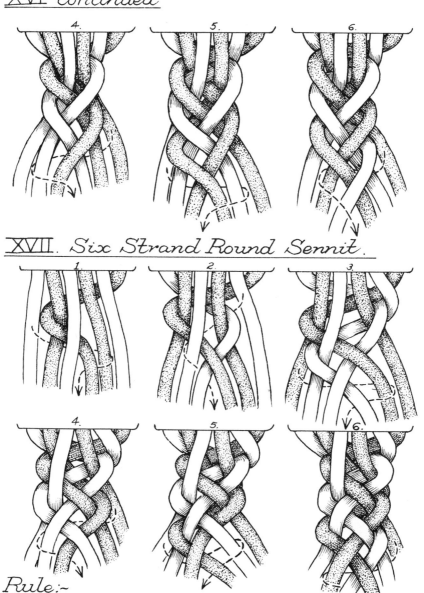

XVII. *Six Strand Round Sennit.*

Rule:-

Outside right to left behind four & to centre over one & under one; outside left to right behind four, & to centre over one & under one, and repeat.

When learning how to make a sennit, it is always worth considering the various combinations of colour, texture and size which may be applicable to the strands being used. Consider also what effect the doubling of certain strands may have. Finally ask yourself whether you might effectively introduce a completely different material into your sennit, such as a piece of ribbon, leather, plastic or even brightly plated wire.

5　Multi-strand combination knots

Some of the knots described in this Chapter appear rather daunting at first glance, but, taken step-by-step, as illustrated, carefully completing each step in turn, they are straightforward and no more difficult than many of the knots previously described. Indeed, most of these knots are produced by combining the simple multi-strand knots in various ways. When tying knots of this kind, bear in mind that the strands should lie in their places easily. It is no good pushing and poking at a strand which apparently does not want to lie where you want it. Try twisting it a little, first one way and then, if it is still recalcitrant, try the other way. Almost invariably an awkward strand will lie down peacefully if it is twisted the right amount in the right direction, whereas pushing, poking and even hammering will have no effect whatever.

For practising these knots, braided nylon line of the kind sold by Woolworth's for clothes line is ideal, because it is easy to work with and can be repeatedly tied and untied, without any appreciable wear. Several of the illustrations in this Chapter show the knots tied in three strand laid rope, as they well may be, but they can be tied equally well with four or more strands, perhaps from a sennit, although if more than five strands are used, it will be necessary to work over a core.

Wall and Crown Knot
This is always known as the Wall and Crown, although the Crown is tied first and the Wall below it afterwards. The knot is usually doubled, as illustrated,

77

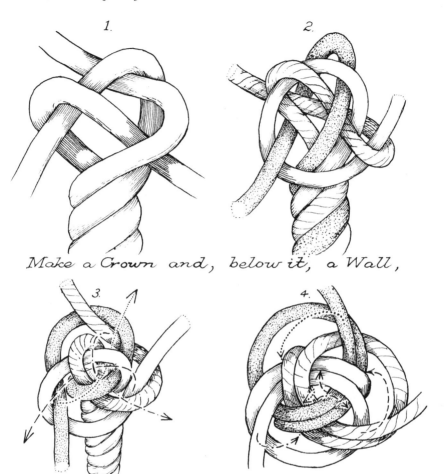

Make a Crown and, below it, a Wall,

double the lead & pass the ends up through the centre.

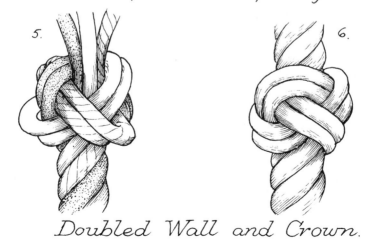

Doubled Wall and Crown.

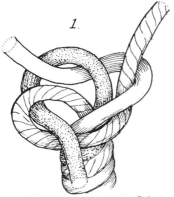

1.

2.

Make a Wall,   *double above the lead.*

3.

4.

doubled Wall   *make a Crown above,*

tuck the ends down through the Wall and

cut them off close.

5.

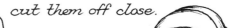

6.

Wall Rose Knot.

or tripled, by simply following the lead of the original knot around again. A doubled Wall and Crown is often tied with the ends after an eye splice made in a whistle or knife lanyard, to provide a decorative finish instead of leaving the cut ends protruding. Each strand has been given a different shading in the drawings to make the sequence easier to follow.

Wall Rose Knot

This is often simply called *the* Rose Knot, because it was probably the first of a whole series of knots which may be thought to resemble the flower. All of the Rose Knots are terminal knots, and several of them make attractive buttons, this being one.

Matthew Walker Rose Knots

The similarity between these Rose Knots and the Wall Rose Knot is close, as is the relationship of the Matthew Walker to the Wall. The single Matthew Walker, with or without the doubled Crown, makes a better button than does the double Matthew Walker, the latter producing too deep a knot for this purpose.

Diamond Rose Knot

Known also as the Rosenkopf (German for Rose Head), this is a very elegant terminal knot, and, of all the Rose Knots, the one which for most people bears the closest resemblance to the flower.

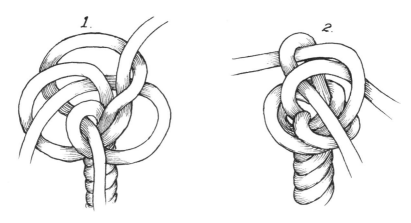

Tie a Single Matthew Walker, above it a Crown,

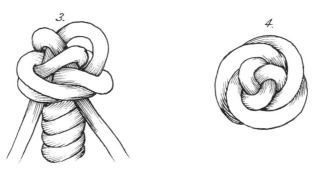

tuck the ends down and cut them off close beneath.

Matthew Walker Rose Knots.

*Starting with a Double Matthew Walker
produces this deeper knot of similar plan.*

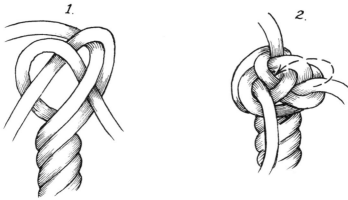

Tie a Crown, below it a Single Matthew Walker

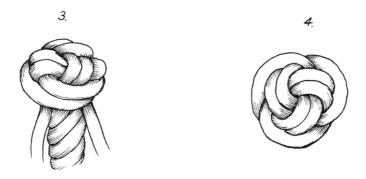

double the Crown, tuck the ends down through the centre and cut them off close underneath.

A Double Matthew Walker below the doubled Crown as above produces this knot.

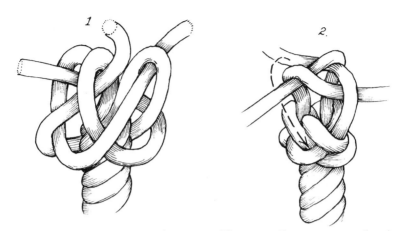

Tie a Diamond with a Crown above,

double the whole knot above the lead,
tuck the ends down through the centre,

and cut the ends off close underneath.

Diamond Rose Knot.

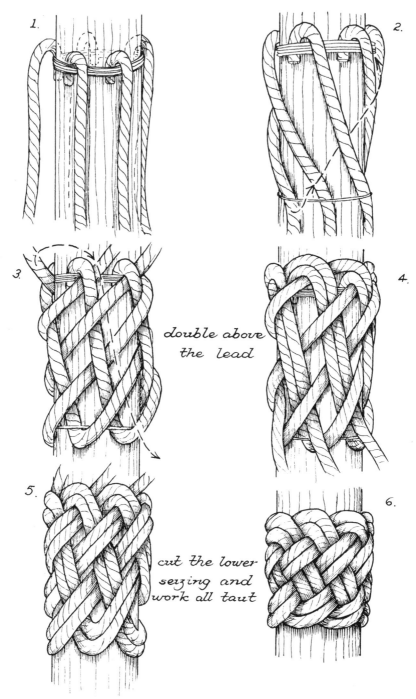

1.

2.

3.

*double above
the lead*

4.

5.

*cut the lower
seizing and
work all taut*

6.

Extended   Diamond   Knot.

Extended Diamond Knot

Multi-strand knots of this type are usually tied over a core or base, as illustrated, being tubular in form. Note the close resemblance of the completed knot to a five lead, five bight Turk's Head; indeed, this type of knot and the extended Wall and Crown, which follows, are often called multi-strand Turk's Heads. An additional pair of leads can be added to the knot by simply tucking each strand over and under once more at stage 2 of the illustrated sequence. The number of bights in the completed knot is the same as the number of strands employed to make it. Many other variations of the extended Diamond, and the extended Wall and Crown, are possible by varying the lead up from the lower seizing (diagram 2 of the extended Diamond sequence). Instead of leading each strand up over one and under one alternately, the lead could be over two and under two; alternatively under two, over two and under two. Three further possibilities are illustrated on the next page, but do not imagine that these are the only possible variations.

The more tucks there are in the lead up from the lower seizing, the more extended the finished knot becomes, and the number of possible variations in design increases.

If a large number of strands is used, it is not advisable to lead them all out of the knot at the same tuck, as illustrated in diagram 5 of the Extended Diamond sequence, because doing so will cause a bulge around the circumference at the edge of the knot from which the ends are cut off. To avoid this, cut the upper seizing after completing the knot, and continue tucking some ends further into the knot, withdrawing the parallel, originally seized, ends, in the same lead to maintain the doubled appearance. Scatter the ends at different tucks throughout the knot, as shown in diagram 4a of the following sequence illustrating the extended Wall and Crown.

Start as Extended Diamond Knot diagrams 1 & 2.

Lead up from lower seizing :~   under one,
over two, under one, & double above the lead.

Lead up from lower seizing :~   under two,
over one, under two, & double above the lead.

Lead up :~ under one, over one, under two,
over one, under one, & double above the lead.

Variations of the Extended Diamond.

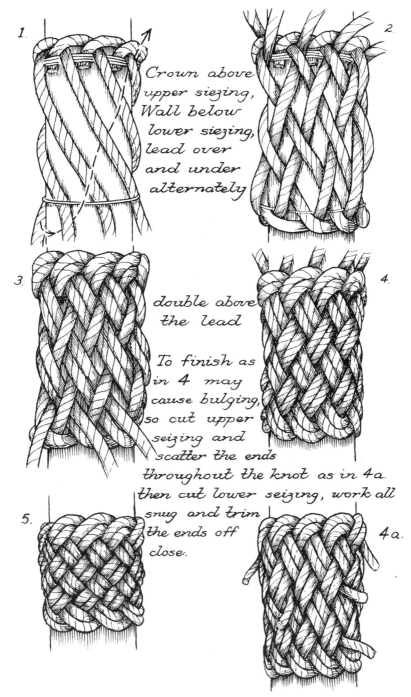

1.

2.

Crown above upper siezing, Wall below lower siezing, lead over and under alternately

3.

4.

double above the lead

To finish as in 4 may cause bulging, so cut upper seizing and scatter the ends throughout the knot as in 4a. then cut lower seizing, work all snug and trim the ends off close.

5.

4a.

Extended Wall and Crown.

Extended Wall and Crown Knots

This is a technique very similar to that described for the extended Diamond Knot, the difference being in the extra tucks due to the Crown above the upper seizing and the Wall below the lower seizing. The possible design variations are equally numerous and are produced in the same ways, the principle one being by varying the lead of the strands up from the lower seizing, or the Wall below it. Still more design permutations in the Wall and Crown and Diamond extended knots are possible by giving alternate strands different leads. This is illustrated in the first three diagrams of the next sequence of drawings, in which six strands are shown, three of which lead up from the Wall over one, under two, over two, under one, whereas the alternate three strands lead up over two, under one, over one, under two. This technique is only possible with an even number of strands. With a large number of strands, having a suitable factor, it is possible to extend the repetition of a sequence of different leads over three or even more strands; for instance, every third strand might be tucked over one and under three, the strands next to and to the right of those already tucked being tucked over two and under two, and the remaining third of the strands in this sequence of three being tucked over three and under one.

Obviously to produce such a design a minimum of six, but preferably nine or twelve strands, is required, otherwise the repetition of the sequence, and therefore the design itself, is not readily apparent.

The final three diagrams in this sequence of variations illustrate how the design possibilities of these knots are affected primarily by the sections of strands which appear on the surface of the knot, passing over rather than under other strands. In the illustrated knot, each strand is led up from the Wall below the lower seizing, over one, under one, over two, under one, over three and under one. Usually knots of this type are tied so that they are symmetrical in all dimensions; however, as this illustration shows, they do not have to be, and, in some situations, provide opportunities for extending design permutations even further.

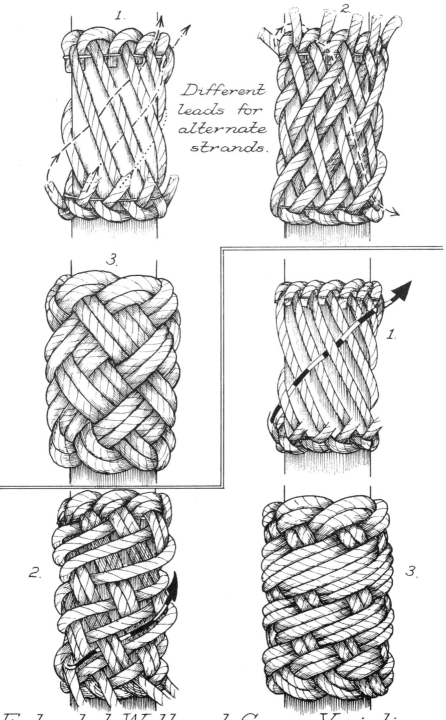

Different leads for alternate strands.

Extended Wall and Crown Variations.

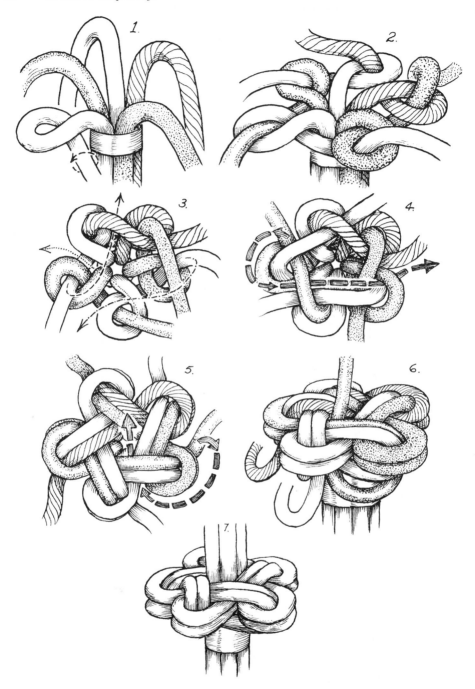

Five Strand Star Knot.

Five Strand Star Knot

Star Knots can be tied with a minimum of three strands, and there is theoretically no upper limit to the number of strands employed. In practice, however, Star Knots of less than five strands are unusual, and if more than five strands are employed, they are tied over a core. The Star Knot is unique, and probably the most difficult knot of all, being regarded as the summit of achievement in this field. In fact it is not really difficult, providing that it is tied with patience and that each step is carefully completed in turn. Each succeeding step produces a stage in the knot which is an entity in itself, and which it should be possible to lay down and pick up again without undue disturbance of the construction. The completed steps are shown in diagrams 2, 4 and 5 and the completed knot in diagram 7. In the first step each strand is led up through a round turn in its neighbour. Take particular note of the twist to be imparted to each strand, indicated in diagram 1 by a pecked arrow, in order to produce the round turn through which the following strand passes. The following strand may be pushed up through the round turn in the strand to the right of itself before imparting the required twist for the next round turn. By this means, each succeeding strand is held in place by its predecessor. When every strand has been tucked, the first stage is complete and the knot should have an evenly spaced appearance as in diagram 2. The next step is to tie the strands in a Crown *to the left,* as illustrated in diagram 3, after which stage two is completed and the knot should look from above as diagram 4 of the sequence. Each strand is now led back under itself in the Crown and tucked down through the round turn in the second strand to its right. This step is a little difficult to describe clearly in words, but the lead is clearly shown by broad arrows in diagram 4. When all strands have been tucked down, the third stage is complete, and the knot should appear as in diagram 5. The final step is to tuck each strand in turn up to the left and through the centre of the knot. When this has been done, the completed knot should appear as in diagram 7, and it can be worked taut and even with a pricker or pliers. The ends may be neatly whipped together with a palm and needle whipping, or may be laid up into a rope, or made into a sennit. If the knot is made really tight, there is no reason why the ends should not be cut off close to the knot, if the intention is to use it as a terminal knot, but for this purpose it is probably better to tie a Crown first and tie the Star the other way up.

6 Covering and netting

One of the best uses of fancy ropework in the home is to provide handsome coverings for plain, humdrum and even downright ugly objects, thereby giving the item concerned a new and often different life. Empty jam jars and paste pots can be converted into charming and unique vases; empty bottles, particularly those with an unusual shape or colour, offer wide scope for conversion into lamps; plastic and aluminium tablet tubes make useful needle cases, and so on. Detailed suggestions and designs for a number of such projects will be found in the next chapter; here some of the basic covering methods are described. It is worth noting that some of these covering methods can be mixed or utilised together conveniently, thus providing innumerable design variations.

Coachwhipping
This is simply tying a round sennit over a tubular core, which may be a length of rope, or an item to be decorated. Coachwhipping is often to be seen, even today, used to decorate the large telescope which is kept on a ship's bridge. Usually six or eight strands are as much as one pair of hands can manage, but using two or even three strands together as one will normally allow enough strands to be used to cover the required area with a fairly simple sennit. The illustrated example of twelve strands used in pairs to form a six strand sennit is typical. The ends of the sennit are seized in position and the seizings are usually covered with Turk's Heads, as illustrated on the telescope at the

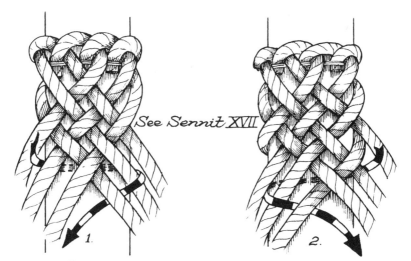

See Sennit XVII

1.   2.

Coachwhipping ~ Six single strands.

1.   2.

Coachwhipping ~ Six double strands.

bottom of page 93. It may be advantageous sometimes to start working from a central seizing, complete the work towards one end and seize it in position at that end. The central seizing can be cast off then and the work completed towards the other end. If the sennit, when completed, does not cover the whole area, the lead may be doubled or tripled using a needle or pricker, but it is usually quite easy to tell whether the number of strands being used will cover the area adequately at an early stage in the work, and adjust the number of strands accordingly.

Cross Pointing

This is the same as Coachwhipping with single strands, but the method of working is different. There should be no need to cover the start and finish, although it will be found necessary to scatter the ends about the length of the knot at the finish, if bulging is to be avoided. The middles of the required number of strands are seized to the core at the top of the area to be covered, each strand being of double the length needed to spiral around the length of the area being covered. The two halves of each strand are then worked as separate strands, as shown in the sequence of drawings. Cross Pointing may be continuous over a considerable length, for instance, it was often used to cover hand rails at the side of a ship's ladders, and in those circumstances the strands were wound onto bobbins to simplify working. Both Coachwhipping and Cross Pointing can be effective using alternate strands of two different colours. The two techniques are not normally used together, being virtually the same when completed, but Cross Pointing is used where Coachwhipping is not possible, due to the large number of strands required.

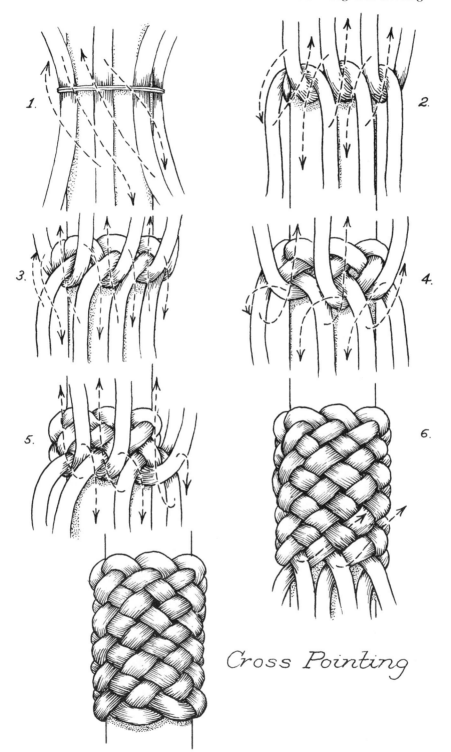

Cross Pointing

Grafting

A covering technique which offers a wide scope for decorative variation, yet which is very simple in principle, Grafting can also be mixed or alternated conveniently with other covering methods, particularly Cross Pointing and Crown Sennit. Basically Grafting is interweaving a 'warp', running continuously around the section being covered, with 'wefts', which run along the length of the section. Diagram 1 of this sequence of diagrams shows the warp passing alternately over and under the wefts in the classic manner of weaving, in which case there must be an even number of wefts. An even number of wefts is also required for the design shown in diagram 3, where the warp takes three turns around the same path before the wefts change places, and also for the design in diagram 5, where the wefts are worked in pairs and the warp is passed twice around the same path. In diagram 2, the warp takes an underhand turn around each weft in sequence, whereas in diagram 4 the warp takes overhand turns in sequence. In diagram 6, it is the wefts which, in sequence, take underhand turns around the warp. Another alternative is for the wefts to take overhand turns around the warp in sequence. To produce the pattern shown in diagram 7 requires the number of wefts to be divisible by both two and three, because the wefts are worked in groups of three, alternating under and over. The first and third weft in each group are crossed to exchange places after every third pass of the warp and the centre weft in each group maintains its line, but always is on the opposite side of the warp from its neighbours. It may be found easier to seize the wefts to the core and apply the warp with a needle, particularly for the patterns in diagrams 2 and 4, but this could not be done in the cases of diagrams 6 and 7, where the wefts do not maintain a constant line. The illustrated examples are only a small sample of the almost unlimited variety of designs possible by Grafting. The technique has this name because it originated as a means of joining, or grafting, two ropes together, but this was a laborious process, involving the careful interweaving of the yarns of the two ends to be joined. The methods used to cover the join or graft have much wider applications and have therefore lived on, although grafting as a means of joining rope is virtually dead, and the name is still used for the covering method.

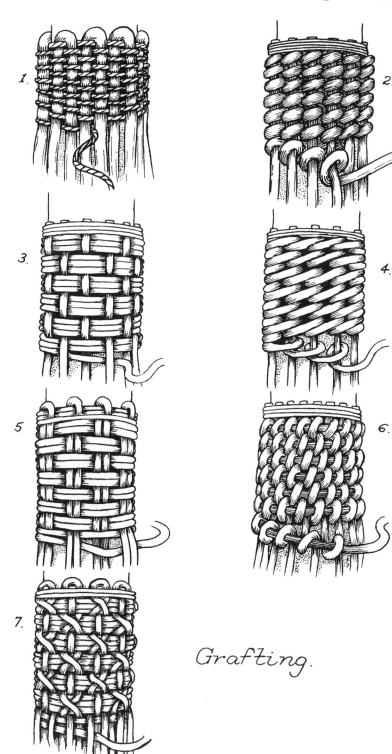

Grafting.

Crown Sennit

This consists of a series of multi-strand Crown knots, made one above, or below, the other. It does not matter whether one works progressively upwards or downwards, as long as the work is kept even, with a constant tension. In the author's opinion it is easier for a right-handed man, working with right-hand laid line, to make Crown Sennit progressing downwards, although it is usually illustrated the other way up. This involves making the Crowns left-handed over the core, as illustrated in sequence B of the drawings. Working in this way the strands can be given a slight twist with their own lay (right-handed), which, in a left-handed Crown, holds them in position, just as left-hand laid strands hold their position in a right-hand laid rope. The converse is also true, of course, so that if working with left-hand laid line, it is best to make right-handed Crowns. If one is working with plaited line, the direction of working is immaterial, but it is still helpful to impart a slight twist to each strand as it is tucked, right-handed if the Crown is being made left-handed and vice-versa. The advantage of using plaited line for Crown Sennit is that one can easily switch direction, from left- to right-handed and back again. Since the pattern produced by Crown Sennit is a spiral, by changing the direction of working, one can change the direction of the spiral and thus produce design variations. Crown Sennit does not otherwise permit much design variation, the pattern being changed primarily by altering the number and colour of the strands employed. One further slight variation is possible by working with every second or every third strand in sequence, but the pattern remains basically very much the same. This technique has one major advantage over others, however, in that virtually any multi-strand knot can be incorporated into the design at will. For instance one may start with a multi-strand Wall and Crown, doubled or tripled, follow with a sequence of Crown Sennit, make a Matthew Walker knot, followed by more Crown Sennit and finish with a Star Knot. Similarly one may incorporate the Diamond Knot and the Footrope Knot within sequences of Crown Sennit, which may also be alternated with Cross Pointing and Grafting.

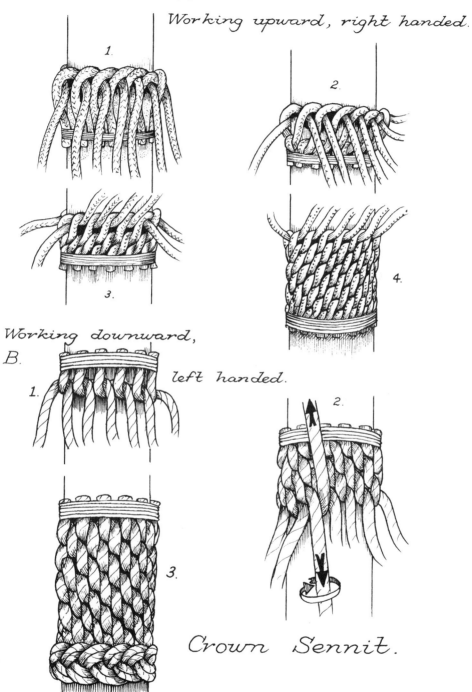

A.

Working upward, right handed.

1.

2.

3.

4.

Working downward,

B.

1.

left handed.

2.

3.

Crown Sennit.

Half-Hitching

Sometimes called Needle Hitching, Half-Hitching is the most versatile covering technique using cordage, because, whereas Coachwhipping and Cross-Pointing can be used only on tubular or cylindrical cores and Grafting also requires its core to have parallel sides at least, Half-Hitching can be made to cover virtually any contour. Normally Half-Hitching is applied with a needle, but, if line too heavy for a needle is desirable, the leading end usually can be adequately stiffened with a few turns of self-adhesive tape. The easiest form of Half-Hitching is the simple spiral stitch shown on the first page of drawings dealing with this method. The whole secret of satisfactory Half-Hitching lies in maintaining even spacing between the stitches. In the first page dealing with Half-Hitching the spacing between stitches is shown deliberately rather wider than is normal practice, in order to make the drawings as clear as possible, and this is also the case in the sequence captioned Covering Contours two pages later; nevertheless this does illustrate that, providing the stitching is even, wide spacing between stitches does not necessarily detract from the decorative effect of the work.

Unless working over a markedly convex surface, the use of a packing needle will be found helpful, as the curved point of this type of needle makes it easier to pick up the previous row of stitching. In extreme cases, an upholstery needle, which is 'U' shaped, can be useful, but these are not easy to handle.

Half-Hitching uses up twine at a remarkable rate, and it is often necessary to join the leading end of a new length of twine to the trailing end of a length already worked. It is worth taking care to do this as neatly as possible, to avoid the join showing up in and spoiling an otherwise good piece of work. If the twine is formed of strands laid up in the conventional way, it is worth taking the trouble to make a proper long-splice to join the new length on. Otherwise probably the best alternative method is a tucked marline splice.

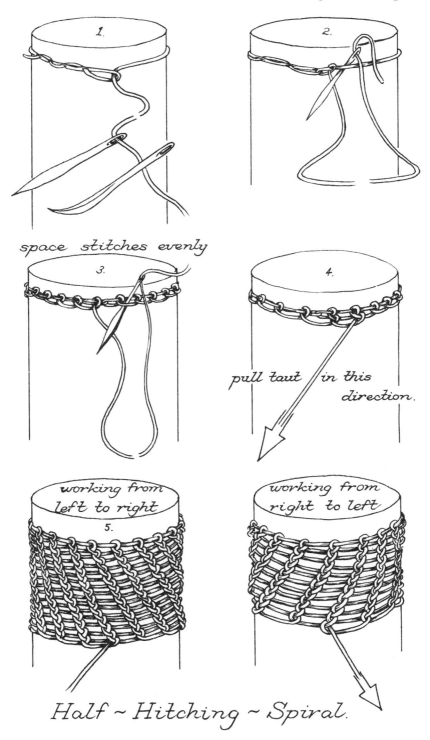

1.

2.

space stitches evenly

3.

4.

pull taut in this direction.

working from left to right

5.

working from right to left

Half ~ Hitching ~ Spiral.

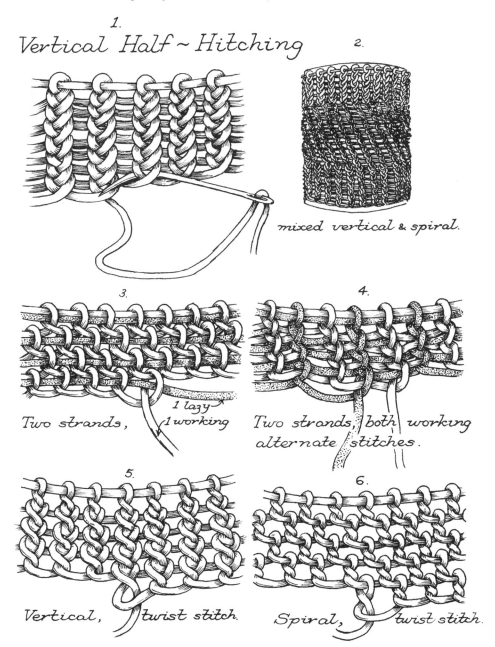

1.
Vertical Half ~ Hitching

2.

mixed vertical & spiral.

3.
Two strands, 1 lazy → / 1 working

4.
Two strands, both working alternate / stitches.

5.
Vertical, *twist stitch.*

6.
Spiral, *twist stitch.*

Half ~ Hitching Variations.

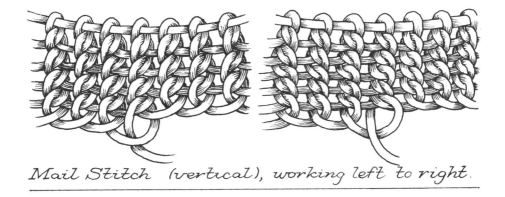

Mail Stitch (vertical), working left to right.

To cover a convex surface

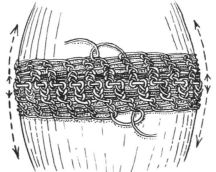

work outwards from the widest section.
When stitches become
crowded, miss out
alternate stitches in
a row.

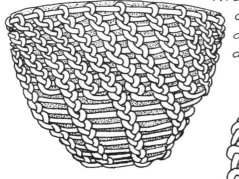

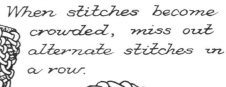

Covering Contours.

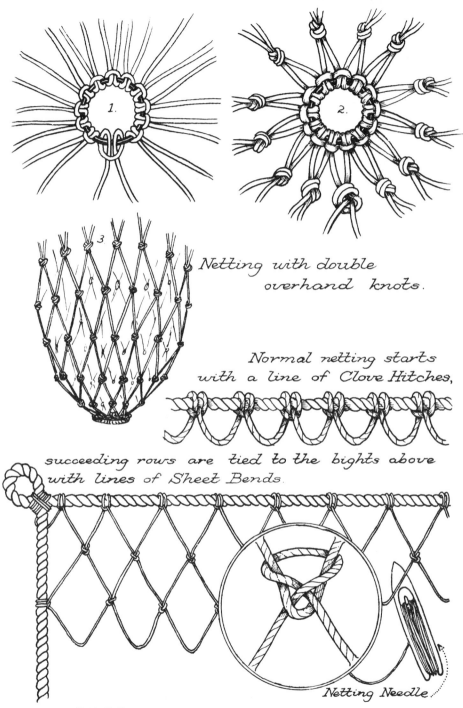

1.

2.

3.

Netting with double overhand knots.

Normal netting starts with a line of Clove Hitches,

succeeding rows are tied to the bights above with lines of Sheet Bends.

Netting Needle

Netting.

Netting

The two commonest types of netting are illustrated first, one being made by double Overhand Knots and the other by Sheet Bends. The Double Overhand Knot method is used mainly for making bags, the start being made by Cow Hitching the middles of doubled strands to a ring, which forms the base of the bag. Diagrams 1, 2 and 3 illustrate this method. Normally a net is started by first making the outline of the proposed net in a heavier line, then along one side of this a row of Clove Hitches, with loops between, is tied using the actual netting material. This provides the top row of the net, and a further Clove Hitch is tied to the boundary line at the side when this is reached. The second and succeeding rows are tied to the top row with Sheet Bends and at the end of each row, a further Clove Hitch is taken around the boundary line. Other knots may be used for netting equally effectively, for instance double Figure of Eight Knots may be used instead of Overhand Knots and, as illustrated on the page captioned Netting Variations, Granny Knots, Reef Knots, or, particularly for decorative effect, Carrick Bends may all be used instead of Sheet Bends. In fact there is much to be said for the Granny Knot in this particular role, if in no other, because unlike the Sheet Bend, a loop can not be pulled through it, and thus distort the mesh. The Sheet Bend is the knot normally used in fishing nets, however, but, if you ever have the opportunity of watching fishing nets being made by hand, you will find, after admiring the incredible speed at which the makers produce netting, that their Sheet Bends are being made upside down; so that instead of having to push the needle up through the preceding loop, around the back of it and then down through the bight, as one does in making a conventional Sheet Bend, they take a half twist in the preceding loop then merely pass the needle up, over and down. The result is a Sheet Bend made from the opposite direction to the normal. If you find this difficult to understand, try turning the illustration of the Sheet Bend Netting upside down.

Conventional netting requires the use of a Netting Needle and these are not easy to find in normal retail outlets, indeed it is doubtful whether the average ship's chandler would stock such a thing these days. However, the shape is relatively simple, as the approximately full-sized illustration shows, and it is not difficult to produce a perfectly adequate netting needle from heavy cardboard, thin plywood, hardboard or a sheet of plastic. Short lengths or small areas of decorative netting, such as might be used to cover a tassel, can be made most conveniently with an ordinary sail needle.

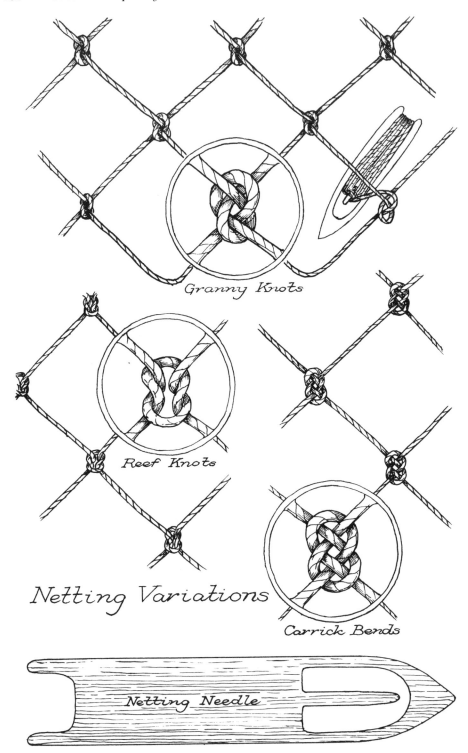

Granny Knots

Reef Knots

Netting Variations

Carrick Bends

Netting Needle

7 Ropecraft design

Having learned all the knots and techniques of ropecraft previously described, it is time to consider the ways in which this acquired skill may be used in designing and producing useful and beautiful objects.

Many of the knots and techniques already discussed have their own obvious uses, for instance, Turk's Heads make admirable scarf and table napkin rings, the Ocean Plait, Prolong Knot and Carrick Bend extensions make excellent mats, and the various sennits can be used to make decorative straps, belts and cords. We want to consider now the less obvious uses of these and other knots and techniques.

It is convenient to observe that most of the covering techniques, such as needle hitching, grafting, cross pointing and crown sennit produce a relatively flat area of decorative knots, which can be used as a background against which to display the more flamboyant and bulky knots. In the photographs of the covered coffee jar and covered brandy bottle, note that most of the surface area of these items is Crown Sennit. The top of the bottle is crowned with a seven point Star Knot, the junction of the neck and body is delineated by a doubled Wall and Crown, the 'waist' is discreetly girdled by a single Matthew Walker knot and the base is completed by a second doubled Wall and Crown. Since the latter is worked over a vertical surface and the knot at the base of the neck is almost horizontal, the repetition of the same knot twice in the design, not normally to be recommended, is not detrimental in this case.

If a heavy line is employed, the bulky knots should be used with more discretion, because the texture of the 'background' becomes more obtrusive as the size of the line increases. For example, study the three lamps together (see frontispiece). Each of these lamps is made in basically the same way (described in detail later in this chapter), but the material used on the centre one is a thicker line of sisal, the left-hand one is covered with a thinner line of braided nylon, and the right-hand lamp is covered with a still thinner three-stranded flax line. Notice that, on the centre lamp, where thick line of hard texture is used, bulky decorative knots are confined to the top and base only. A narrow Matthew Walker knot was sufficient to decorate the centre line of the nylon-covered lamp, whereas the soft and relatively thin flax line allowed the use of a doubled Wall and Crown around the centre line of the right-hand lamp, without making the design too heavily ornate.

If two or more colours are used, the design will not require much additional decoration by way of bulky knots. As an example, look at the photograph of the flask covered by needle hitching. Each side is stitched in quarters of light blue and black, each quarter having been worked separately around its own perimeter and concentrically inward. The cap is covered with a single five lead four bight Turk's Head in braided white nylon and the neck carries a three lead five bight Turk's Head in white nylon twine. To have added any further decoration to the body of the flask would have been excessive.

The 'background' covering techniques may be subdivided conveniently into those which spiral and those which produce straight lines. Crown Sennit invariably spirals, Cross Pointing and Grafting usually produce straight lines, or the equivalent from a design point of view, but Needle Hitching can be varied at will from straight lines to spiral and back again. Examine the photograph of the author's knife and you will find three different 'background' techniques used together on the sheath. From a twelve strand Star knot at the top, Crown Sennit leads down, to terminate in a tripled Wall and Crown, beneath which Needle Hitching starts, spiralling down in the opposite direction to that of the Crown Sennit above it. The final two and a quarter inches of the sheath, which is nine inches in length overall, are covered in vertical Hitching, which balances the part of the knife handle, decorated with a three lead five bight Turk's Head, projecting from the top of the sheath. The 'core' of this sheath was a strong cardboard tube, upon which a reel of line had originally been wound by the manufacturer. The cardboard tube was flattened and shaped to a point at the tip, and given several coats of varnish, inside and out, before being covered.

The 'lumpy' decorative knots can be subdivided for design purposes into three basic categories, the *narrow*, typified by a single Matthew Walker knot, the *wide*, typified by a Double Diamond or Wall and Crown knot, and the *deep*, typified by the Star Knot, which projects outwards from the surface of the work to a greater depth than any other knot of its width. Generally one finds that the most effective design is achieved by alternating these categories and avoiding the use of consecutive knots from the same category. Consider the bell lanyards in the photographs. The one on the left of the pair has a *shallow* single Diamond knot below the eye, then a *deep* six point Star knot; the Crown Sennit below that is broken by a *narrow* Double Matthew Walker knot, below which Crown Sennit again leads into a *wide* doubled Wall and Crown, with a *deep* five point Star terminal knot.

The right-hand Bell Lanyard has a *shallow* but *wide* knot forming the eye, known as a Hangman's Knot, which leads into a fairly *deep* but *narrow* Matthew Walker Rose knot. A plain length of Crown Sennit follows down to a *wide* doubled Wall and Crown above a *deep* six point Star and a *narrow* crowned Matthew Walker Rose terminal knot.

It is no accident that in these Lanyards each consecutive knot is of a different category from that of its predecessor. The same rule applies to the third Bell Lanyard, photographed alone, which is easily made from four strands of braided nylon line, the yarns of which have been brushed out into a tassel at the bottom. To take the kinks out of the yarns, the tassel was held in the steam from the spout of a boiling kettle for a few minutes.

These photographs and the designs of the projects which follow are intended to stimulate the reader to produce new ideas and designs of his or her own. Copy these designs by all means, but as you do so consider how they may be varied and improved, or adapted to other purposes. For instance, we have seen how mats can be made by the Ocean Plait, now imagine two small Ocean Plait mats stitched together all around the edges except at one end. Might that not make a handsome spectacle case?

It is perhaps trite to point out that design is a very personal matter, and that what one person may consider beautiful may be regarded by another as in arrant bad taste, but a warning may be entered here that it is not difficult to over-decorate in the enthusiasm of having new skills to demonstrate. It is always worthwhile making a rough sketch or diagram of what you intend your finished product to look like and stick to that whilst working; do not be tempted to elaborate without careful forethought, for one thing, you may well run out of line before reaching a satisfactory conclusion!

8   Practical projects

PROJECT I—A LANYARD FOR KNIFE OR WHISTLE

A simple lanyard consists of a length of light line, having a large eye spliced in one end and a small eye in the other end, the large eye being placed around the neck of the wearer and the small eye being attached to the whistle, knife, bunch of keys, stop watch or other valuable article, usually by means of a Cow Hitch. The illustration shows two methods of employing the tucked strands after the splice to form decorative knots in the lanyard. Sometimes one sees the larger eye in a lanyard formed by a slip knot, but this is not recommended, because, if the lanyard catches up on something, the slip knot may pull the eye tight around the throat in the manner of a noose.

PROJECT II—A HAMMOCK

The illustration shows one end of the hammock only, both ends being similar. The sides of the hammock are formed by two equal lengths of rope, with eyes spliced in each end. Through the eyes in one end of each length of rope are passed the ends of the bridle for that hammock end, and a reef knot is formed at each eye, as illustrated by the inset. The two ends of the bridle are then spliced together, either by a short splice, or more elegantly by a long splice. The sides of the hammock are held apart by two wooden stretchers, notched at each end to fit the rope, inserted in the bridles. These stretchers can be made conveniently from lengths of broom handle. The web of the hammock is made

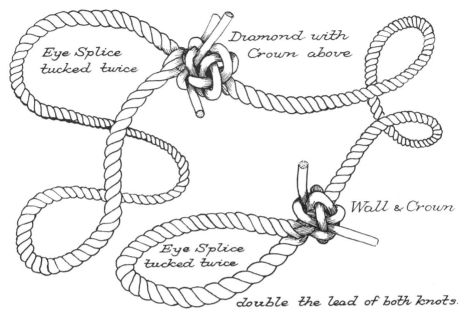

Eye Splice tucked twice

Diamond with Crown above

Wall & Crown

Eye Splice tucked twice

double the lead of both knots.

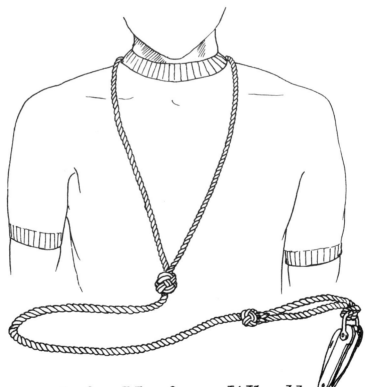

Lanyard for Knife or Whistle.

A Hammock.

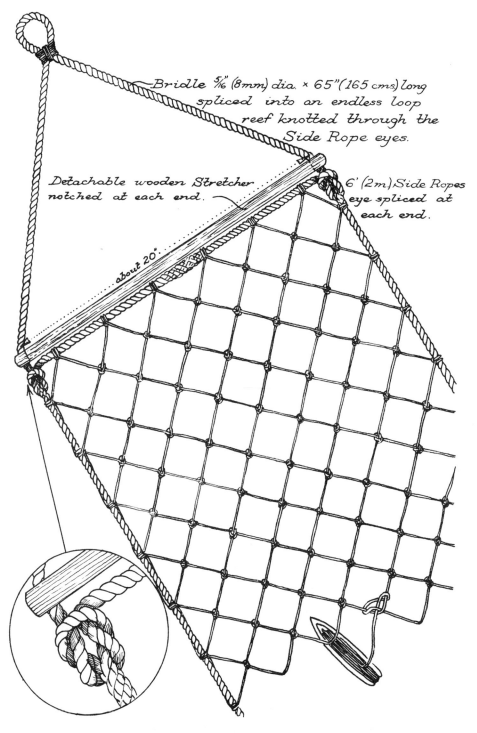

Bridle ⁵⁄₁₆" (8mm) dia. × 65" (165 cms) long spliced into an endless loop reef knotted through the Side Rope eyes.

Detachable wooden Stretcher notched at each end.

about 20"

6' (2m) Side Ropes eye spliced at each end.

by netting between the side ropes, from one end to the other, with a netting needle. The netting can be made by the double overhand knot method, the strands being middled and Cow Hitched to the bridle between the side ropes at one end, but this is a slow method and the length of the strands needed makes them awkward and unwieldy to work with.

PROJECT III—ROPE EDGED TRAY No. 1

The base of the tray may be cut, using a coping saw or jigsaw, from plywood, hardboard or chipboard of a suitable thickness. If the base is to be covered with a washable or heat resistant material, such as Fablon or Formica, it should be done at this stage. The next step is to drill an even number of holes at equidistant intervals about half an inch in from the edge. Through these holes the middled strands are passed as illustrated, so the holes must be of a slightly larger size than the strands to be used. The dimensions stated in the illustration are those of an actual tray made by this method, and are intended as a guide rather than a rule. Any quick setting transparent glue may be used to ensure that the final tuck remains in position, but it is essential to pull the working up as tight as possible first. The names of knots stated against the illustrations for this Project and the next are not, strictly speaking, correctly applicable to the procedure illustrated, but they are used here as descriptive terms to indicate what is intended and as an *aide memoire*.

PROJECT IV—ROPE EDGED TRAY No. 2

This method is best used for a round or oval tray, or anyway one which has well rounded corners, particularly if the line to be used is stiff. It is best to use an easily washable line for trays, made from a synthetic fibre such as poly-ethylene or polypropylene. There are numerous possible variations of these methods, but the two illustrated have been proved satisfactory in use, which is worth knowing when an abortive effort can be costly in both time and materials. Please note also that an excellent picture frame can be made by exactly the same methods; it is merely a matter of removing the centre of the tray!

Rope edged Tray No 1.

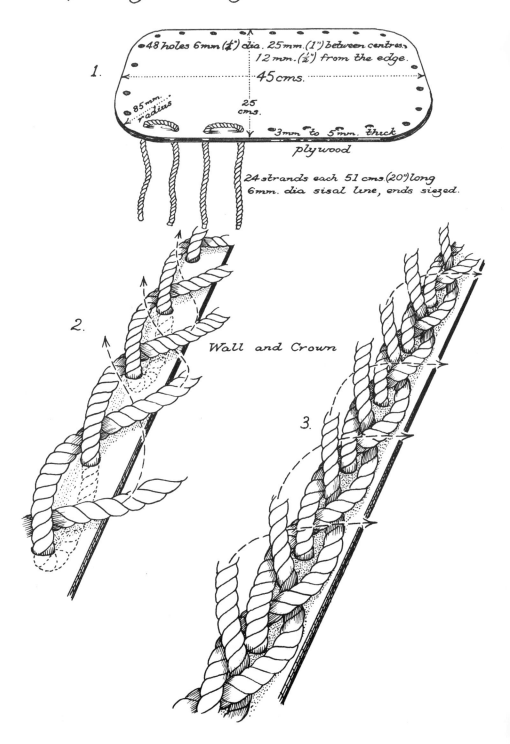

1.
48 holes 6mm (¼") dia. 25mm. (1") between centres. 12 mm. (½") from the edge.
45 cms.
85mm. radius
25 cms.
3mm. to 5mm. thick plywood
24 strands each 51 cms (20") long 6mm. dia sisal line, ends sized.

2.

Wall and Crown

3.

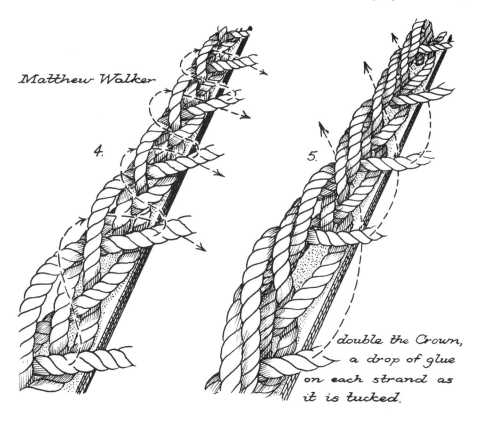

Matthew Walker

4.

5.

double the Crown,
a drop of glue
on each strand as
it is tucked.

When the glue is dry, cut the ends off close on the inside.

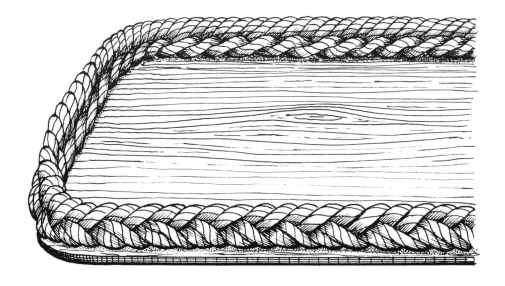

Rope edged
Tray Nº 2.

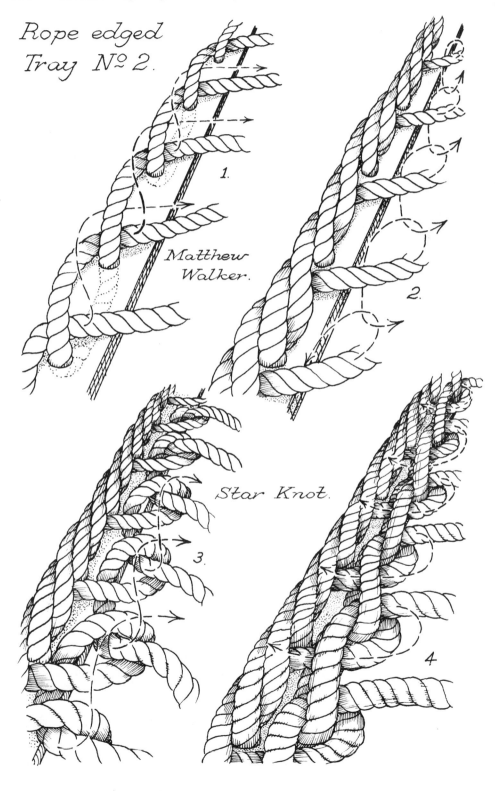

1.

Matthew
Walker.

2.

Star Knot.

3.

4

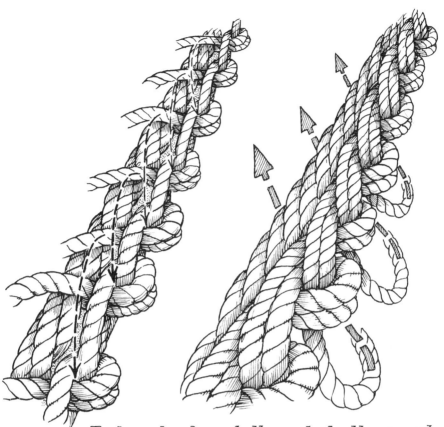

Tuck each strand through to the inside
with a drop of glue and cut off neatly.

PROJECT V—TABLE LAMP

The author has made scores of lamps based upon this design, and the range of possible variations is very wide. For instance where Crown Sennit is indicated, Grafting will do equally well, and one may substitute a Rose Knot for the Star, a Star for the Matthew Walker, and so on. The materials are easily obtained and little woodworking skill is needed to cut a short length of broom handle and a circular base, and drill a few holes. If difficulty is anticipated in drilling a hole right through the centre of the broom handle section, this is not essential. So long as a hole about an inch deep is drilled in the top, into which the brass nipple for the lampholder is screwed, a hole into this can be drilled through the side at the top for the flex wire to pass through, and the wire can be led from there down the outside of the broom handle section, held in place with a couple of pieces of sticky tape. The ropework is then almost completed, the wire being brought out through the working near the base. As the materials are all non-conducting, this design is perfectly safe electrically.

PROJECT VI—DOOR KNOCKER

This design, like all the others, is capable of wide variation and, if the Large Star Knot is omitted, or replaced by a wide but shallow knot, an attractive handle or becket, as often found on old sea chests, can be produced. The door knocker illustrated was given two coats of epoxy resin after completion, to make it hard and weather-proof, but several coats of varnish or even paint would do as well.

Table Lamp.

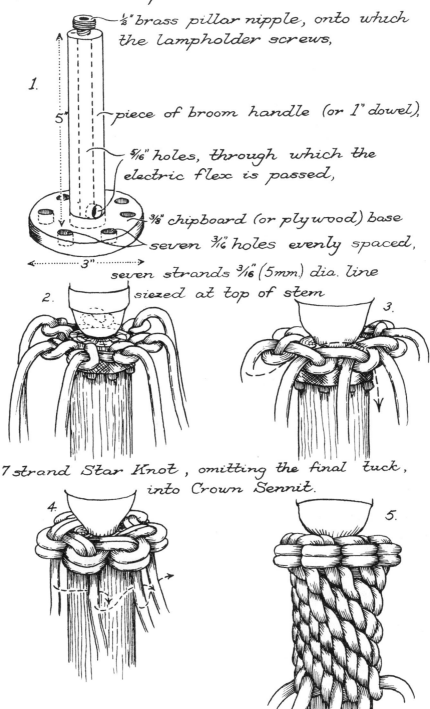

½" brass pillar nipple, onto which the lampholder screws,

1.

5"

piece of broom handle (or 1" dowel),

5⁄16" holes, through which the electric flex is passed,

⅜" chipboard (or plywood) base

seven ³⁄₁₆" holes evenly spaced,

3"

seven strands ³⁄₁₆" (5mm.) dia. line siezed at top of stem

2.

3.

7 strand Star Knot, omitting the final tuck, into Crown Sennit.

4.

5.

6.

Halfway down, a Matthew Walker,

7.

a flat doubled Wall & Crown over the base,

8.

the ends are tucked down through the holes in the base with a drop of glue, and cut off flush.

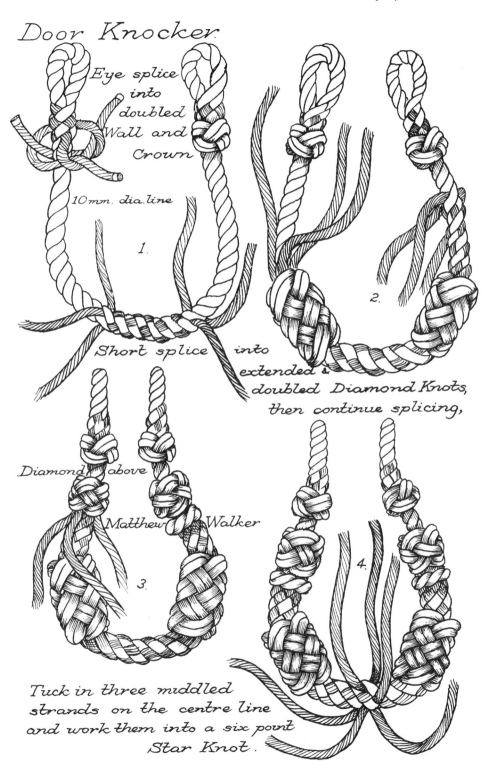

Door Knocker.

Eye splice into doubled Wall and Crown

10 mm. dia. line

1.

Short splice   into extended & doubled Diamond Knots, then continue splicing,

2.

Diamond above

Matthew   Walker

3.

4.

Tuck in three middled strands on the centre line and work them into a six point Star Knot.

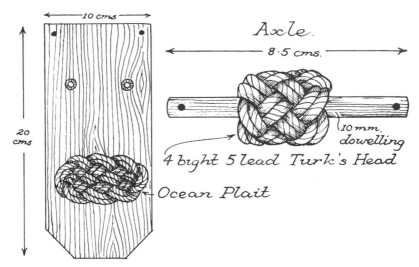

Mounting Board of
10 ~ 12 mm. plywood.

Axle.

8·5 cms.

10 mm.
dowelling

4 bight 5 lead Turk's Head

Ocean Plait

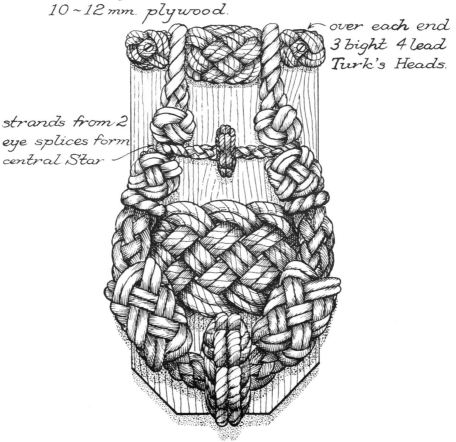

over each end
3 bight 4 lead
Turk's Heads.

strands from 2
eye splices form
central Star

PROJECT VII—CUFF LINKS

Obviously there are innumerable ways in which cuff links can be made using suitable twine and decorative knots; the method illustrated is just one which has proved satisfactory. Almost any kind of twine will do for this purpose, but one criterion must be met, namely that one end of the completed cuff link is small enough to pass through a normal shirt's cuff holes, therefore it is a good idea to make sure of this by testing at an early stage.

The cuff link illustrated has a small wooden toggle at one end, which measures about 2cm. long by about 5.5mm. maximum diameter. These little toggles are easily made from standard 6mm. wooden dowelling, which can be obtained at any 'Do-it-yourself' shop for a few pence. It is usually sold by the foot in lengths up to about six feet. The easiest way, if you have an electric drill available, is to cut off about three inches of the dowelling, secure one end of this short length in the drill chuck, and place the drill horizontally in a vice. Start the drill and shape two toggles from the spinning length of dowelling by holding against it a suitable file, finishing with glass paper, and parting the toggles off with a small saw. A hand drill will do the job just as well, but it is necessary to persuade a helper to turn the handle for you.

Toggles are not essential, of course, because both ends of the cuff link can be made from suitable knots, if preferred. However, it is not an easy matter to tie complicated knots in small twine, as one must if the knots are to be small enough to pass through a shirt button hole. The splices around the toggles are best made by using a large needle to tuck each strand. When tying the Crown, keep it as even as possible, bearing in mind that it is, by itself, too large to be stable. Once backed by the Star, however, the Crown holds its form perfectly well. A clear polyurethane varnish or lacquer—even clear nail varnish will do—gives the completed work a good hard-wearing finish. Other knots well suited to cuff links include the Rose knots, Matthew Walker and Manrope Knots.

Cuff Links.

secure the splice
with masking tape
and tie a

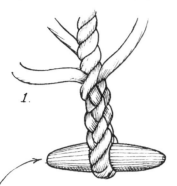

1.

Toggles made from 6mm.
dia. wooden dowelling.

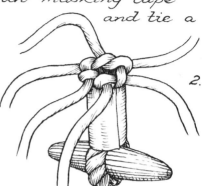

2.

six strand Crown

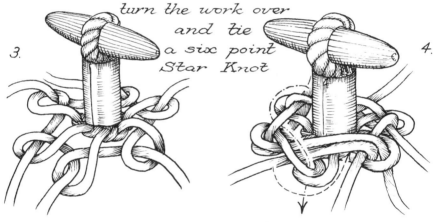

3.

turn the work over
and tie
a six point
Star Knot

4.

cut the ends off close after working all taut,
remove the masking tape and apply varnish.

5.

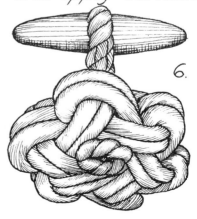

6.

(Drawn greatly magnified).

Conclusion and bibliography

In conclusion the reader is again urged to use his or her imagination freely to invent new designs and uses for ropecraft. Although it is an ancient art, there are many modern applications for it yet to be found. Consider too all kinds of material which may be or may become available for its possible use as an alternative to, or in conjunction with, conventional cordage. Only in this way can the old knots and techniques survive outside a museum case.

Be reminded also that this book cannot be regarded as a comprehensive treatise on the subject of ropecraft, being intended as an introduction and a stimulus of interest among those who enjoy using their hands but have never before considered rope as an art medium. Other books currently available on this subject which may be found helpful are:

The Ashley Book of Knots published in the United Kingdom by Faber and Faber, but originally written and published in the U.S.A. thirty years ago; consequently certain information contained in it is outdated. Nevertheless, this is the only readily available book which approaches a comprehensive treatment of the subject, for which reason it is large in both dimension and price.

The Harrison Book of Knots published by Brown, Son and Ferguson of Glasgow in 1964 concentrates almost exclusively upon the craft as applied to Bell Lanyards, but it is neither expensive nor large and describes one or two interesting and original techniques.

The Encyclopaedia Britannica, in common with other encyclopaedias, contains a short section on knots and references to further bibliography, which is not easy to obtain.

Index